COUPLE CEO

"*CoupleCEO* is a goldmine of information for couples who have a business and want to keep the romance alive. The authors are also the real deal—successful, wealthy, insightful, and in love. I enjoyed reading the book and found that it instantly inspired me. This is a book and an idea whose time has come."

—**Daniel Priestley**, entrepreneur and author of
Key Person of Influence and *Entrepreneur Revolution*

"Very few couples have managed to work together side by side on a daily basis and achieve tremendous success in their business as well as maintain a loving marriage. If you are trying to figure out your next step as a couple, both personally and professionally, Heidi and Scott provide a wealth of unique and valuable insights in their timely new book."

—**Stephen Lesavich**, PhD, JD,
co-author of the award-winning book *The Plastic Effect: How Urban Legends Influence the Use and Misuse of Credit Cards*

"Juggling careers, kids, and everyday crises is not easy for any couple. This book gives helpful guidance that every couple CEO will find useful."

—**Bob Buckhorn**, Mayor

"Throughout CoupleCEO: From the Bedroom to the Boardroom and Back, Scott & Heidi remind us that our relationship and personalities shape our business, not the other way around."

—**Pam Iorio**, president and CEO
Big Bothers Big Sisters of America

"Don't let the title trick you (it isn't a salacious Harlequin Romance), but ironically the tips and strategies you are about to discover are salaciously good. This book will help you and your spouse be CEOs and have an amazing life—Scott and Heidi are proof."

—**Mike Michalowicz**, author of *Profit First*

"*CoupleCEO* offers a comprehensive, integrated approach for entrepreneurial couples to lead successful businesses and live fulfilling lives. The book's breezy, engaging style is like having a conversation with Scott and Heidi: real people with a real contribution. This book offers the wisdom to lead, live, and love your business and life as a CoupleCEO."

—**Susan S. Freeman**, founder and president of Step Up Leader

"Scott and Heidi wandered into my office and asked a few questions about writing a book. They spoke with passion about their desire to help other couples working together as they did, combining their personal and professional life. And now their book is a reality. Am I a proud mother? You know I am."

—**Elaine Fantle Shimberg**, author of twenty-four books

COUPLE CEO

FROM THE BEDROOM TO THE BOARDROOM AND BACK

Scott & Heidi
SHIMBERG

NEW YORK

COUPLE CEO
FROM THE BEDROOM TO THE BOARDROOM AND BACK

Published in New York, New York, by Morgan James Publishing. Morgan James and The Entrepreneurial Publisher are trademarks of Morgan James, LLC. www.MorganJamesPublishing.com

The Morgan James Speakers Group can bring authors to your live event. For more information or to book an event visit The Morgan James Speakers Group at www.TheMorganJamesSpeakersGroup.com.

Scriptures are taken from THE HOLY BIBLE, NEW INTERNATIONAL VERSION®, NIV® Copyright © 1973, 1978, 1984, 2011 by Biblica, Inc.® Used by permission. All rights reserved worldwide.

Myers-Briggs Type Indicator, Myers-Briggs, and MBTI are trademarks or registered trademarks of the MBTI Trust, Inc. in the United States and other countries.

A **free** eBook edition is available with the purchase of this print book.

ISBN 978-1-63047-288-7 paperback
ISBN 978-1-63047-290-0 eBook
ISBN 978-1-63047-289-4 hardcover
Library of Congress Control Number:
2014941483

CLEARLY PRINT YOUR NAME ABOVE IN UPPER CASE

Instructions to claim your free eBook edition:
1. Download the BitLit app for Android or iOS
2. Write your name in **UPPER CASE** on the line
3. Use the BitLit app to submit a photo
4. Download your eBook to any device

Cover Design by:
Chris Treccani
www.3dogdesign.net

Interior Design by:
Bonnie Bushman
bonnie@caboodlegraphics.com

In an effort to support local communities, raise awareness and funds, Morgan James Publishing donates a percentage of all book sales for the life of each book to Habitat for Humanity Peninsula and Greater Williamsburg.

Get involved today, visit
www.MorganJamesBuilds.com.

Habitat
for Humanity®
Peninsula and
Greater Williamsburg
Building Partner

This book is dedicated to all of the couples who choose to discover life's balance, explore life's beauty, and cherish life's sunrises and sunsets . . . for forever and a day.

CONTENTS

Preface
WAYPOINTS

A journey of a thousand miles begins with a single step.
—Confucius

This book is a waypoint in our journey, a milestone in our path as a couple that serendipitously discovered a combined whole far greater than the sum of us each individually. Over the past twenty years, we have developed, built, and sold more than a quarter of a billion dollars in real estate. We've played vital roles in developing a children's museum and creating new residential neighborhoods, enjoying all aspects of the design, development, construction, and community leadership. We're proud of these accomplishments and receive pleasure from driving by these communities, a lasting legacy, watching future generations of people living and playing there. But what provides us with the most satisfaction is realizing that we accomplished this while maintaining a family lifestyle filled with fun, family dinners, travel, and true intimacy.

We know that many entrepreneurial couples struggle to find the balance that can provide a profitable business and a passionate and fulfilled lifestyle. Over the years, people often have asked us how we do it. How do we work together all day and then enjoy being together in the evening and manage to be smiling most of the time?

CoupleCEO™ began in our boardroom, a natural birthplace, as we were strategizing about some new entrepreneurial concepts. We asked ourselves what would be a business that could incorporate everything we're passionate about? Our whiteboard quickly filled with sailing, parenting, traveling, bucket list goals, eating right, entrepreneurship, and fitness.

We began to realize that these passions were giving us a framework, a foundation, in which to effectively and successfully operate as a couple in all aspects of our lives. We were integrating a family business and marital intimacy with all of the fulfillment life mixes in. Living life as a CoupleCEO was our answer to the question "How do you do it?"

Our business grew out of answering that question. We realized couples that live the entrepreneurial life together require a unique set of skills. We pondered how satisfying it would be to share our experiences and help others enjoy the fulfilled life we have cherished.

The life of a CoupleCEO can be exhausting and trying at times. You don't leave the office and go home; it is with you 24/7. Emergencies arise, and you have to be ready to respond. Financial downturns happen, and you have to adjust quickly, or the consequences can be devastating for you, your family, and your employees. We have lots of lessons we have learned over the years and little things that we do subconsciously that we believed if we chronicled and put a framework around, we could help others. It can be quite stressful on relationships to try to create a balancing act among effective communication, intimacy, and health.

Along the way, we have accumulated degrees, certifications, and licenses, such as MBA, MBTI®-certified, licensed building contractor, and licensed real estate broker. But our true expertise comes from the lessons we've learned over the years, the real world experiences as a couple, and the stories that have brought us closer. All of these things are blended together to help build the framework around what we call CoupleCEO. This was arrived at not only from our perspective, but also through extensive research and interviews with dozens of happy, successful entrepreneurial couples.

It's gratifying to know that there are a lot of couples that are successful in their business and enjoying their lifestyle. And there are a lot of couples that want to go from good to great. Commonalities were revealed. Similar themes emerged. They enjoy a healthy, active lifestyle. They clearly understood the strengths and weaknesses of each other and spoke of them candidly, often with anecdotes. They have rules or parameters about times for no business talk. Intimacy is an integral part of their lives, and we observed it through smiles and gentle touches. Our book builds a framework that you, as a couple, can simply and easily implement in your lives to begin to find the balance to enjoy your fulfilled lifestyle as a CoupleCEO.

There are many books and seminars providing guidance to couples that need counseling in their lives. We're not licensed therapists or coaches. Nor are we nutritionists or fitness experts. We're speaking to you from the voice of a CoupleCEO. We sleep, eat, and work together. We've raised our children together and care for our aging parents together. We have had businesses that have done quite well and other ventures that were not successful. We have looked at our businesses and had to analyze if they are sustainable for our lifestyle. As a CoupleCEO, we want to inspire and educate you, the entrepreneurial couple, to live a successful life, where your business and your relationship can coexist and thrive.

We hope you enjoy your journey from the bedroom to the boardroom and back.

Chapter 1

SUNRISE AT HALEAKALĀ

Someday you will find the one who will watch every sunrise with you until the sunset of your life.

—Unknown

She doesn't know what's about to happen, he thought to himself. He lay in the hotel bed beside her, watching her sleeping. The alarm clock said 3 a.m., but it felt like 8 a.m.—the time difference was on their side in Hawaii. They were 4,624 miles from Tampa, Florida, but he felt so at home with her, lying here, waiting to wake up to a brand-new day. He knew this day would end far different from how it had begun, as his stomach tightened, either from nerves or early morning hunger pangs. He gently woke her from her dreams.

Their instructions told them to meet in the lobby by 3:30 a.m. The van arrived as promised to pick them up. Joining other brave souls in the predawn blackness, they stepped into the van that would take them to their final destination. The greetings from the other half-asleep passengers were mostly in nods and smiles.

The vehicle cut through the predawn blackness of the Maui early morning, the road twisting and turning as they made their ascent. She rested her head on his shoulder, and held his right hand. He caressed her left hand, finger by finger, and he closed his eyes, thinking. Practicing. He could feel his heart, a solid pounding rhythm like a bass drum—but could she feel how strongly it was beating?

The van reached the summit of Haleakalā National Park, with an elevation of 10,023 feet. As they stepped out of the vehicle, surrounded by darkness and cold, the only visible light revealed itself from above. They looked skyward, seeing the Milky Way everywhere. And so close. Like the view from a planetarium, an amazing display of stars, planets, the moon, and many other celestial bodies spread out in the heavens. As they viewed the sight above them, they both knew that this would be a memory for a lifetime.

The House of the Sun Visitors Center stood fifty yards behind them. He turned from his sky gaze, looked into her eyes, and announced he'd be right back. He turned and walked toward the visitor's center. Once safely behind a bathroom stall, he reached into his jacket pocket and took out the box. He opened it to take one last look, closed it, and returned it to the warmth of his jacket. He looked into the mirror by the wash basin, looking at a face both terrified and excited, realizing that this sunrise would awaken so much more than just a brand-new day. He smiled as he thought about the beginnings of this brand-new life, an awakening about to appear over the rim of the Haleakalā Crater. With one more deep breath, he left to rejoin his new partner.

She Said "Yes"

At precisely 6:16 a.m. May 10, 1996, as the sun rose over the rim of the crater, he reached into his Windbreaker pocket and turned to her, the light just breaking over her hair, casting a fantastic halo surrounding her head. He spoke to her as if it were the most natural thing he had ever done, offering her the ring he had held in his pocket since leaving Tampa the morning before.

"As the sun's rising over the rim of this crater, I want us to be together, forever and a day."

Whether it was the effect of the Milky Way, or the ten-thousand-foot altitude, or just the reciprocating love that is the foundation of great things to come, she said "yes," and Scott and Heidi's journey together began.

Now, most journeys have their ups and downs, but this one started downhill, literally. As they mounted their bicycles and began a wonderful downhill descent, their tour followed through the switchbacks, Haleakalā Ranch, and the Kula Lavender Flower Farm, continued into the towns of Makawao and Paia and down to the Pacific Ocean, and ended at Paia Bay Beach Park. As they relished the exhilaration of the morning's events, they coasted downhill, viewing Hawaii's lush countryside, inhaling the excitement for this new day and their life together.

As they arrived back at the hotel, Scott grinned, "Well, it's amazing everything you can accomplish by 10:30 in the morning.

We got engaged, biked down a crater ten thousand feet, and explored all of Maui."

Heidi smiled. "Well, I guess we earned our breakfast!"

They sat side by side on their balcony, drinking the rich Kona coffee, watching the butterflies in the garden below. Scott and Heidi thought about the life they were now beginning together, a life comfortably and completely defined by "us" and "we," a life full of new possibilities emerging from a combined whole far greater than the sum of the contributions of each. Together their journey would strive toward fulfillment of dreams, goals, and visions to be achieved by a proper partnership. Both individual accomplishments and shared encouragement would grow together with a blossoming realization of the success that would be, a beautiful synergy of both of their energies and talents.

Years later, they would look back on this moment and cherish the simplicity of the feeling—two young souls coming together for a life filled with all that happens after the sunrise. Their entire journey would not be just an easy downhill ride, nor would it be ever-present coasting with luscious scenery constantly going by. But in sharing their journey together, sharing "forever and a day," they would climb aboard Life's Ride, making their highs more balanced and their lows more kind.

Building their foundation solid and strong, their gifts to the world would become more meaningful and their work, more fulfilling. Scott and Heidi would come to realize a complete life where all the pieces fit together. They would build companies that reflect who they are and what they want to say to the world. They would stand at the helm of their ship, traveling not just toward a destination, but also along a journey that would do great things, touch people along the way, and contribute back. Like a heart that beats as it feeds each capillary, their relationship would continue to supply the sustenance to motivate and invigorate their life's calling.

Chapter 2

THE JOURNEY

It is good to have an end to journey toward; but it is the journey that matters, in the end.

—Ernest Hemingway

rand Cru glistened with the morning dew. As sailboats go, she was a perfect combination of cruising comfort, steady speed, and seaworthy safety. Like a familiar family member, she was a bit high-maintenance, but loved just the same.

Scott and Heidi walked down the dock of the marina to the last slip on the south side toward the vessel, their second home. Their coffee tumblers were filled with the morning dose, his black and hers lightly creamed and sweetened. They approached their sailboat. It was a reflection of them, a deep, stable keel, comfortable and inviting inside, filled with memories both created and enjoyed, as well as those yet to be found.

Grand Cru served as a floating metaphor for enjoying the journey as much as, if not more than, the actual destination. Throughout the years, that journey had sailed through Bahamian island chains, The Florida Keys, Southwestern Florida ports of call, and even nearby St. Petersburg for weekend getaways. Sailing adventures had always filled their children's youth, from crawling infants finding their sea legs along with their first steps, to older children deploying dinghy rides ashore, conquering the next island explorations. Stargazing and s'mores, movies and travel menorahs, soccer balls in the sand, and hanging out at the bow as the wind and the waves and the dolphins joined in. Heidi always said that their family sailing adventures were the most familial times they had, down to the basics of simply enjoying their family in the new surroundings that each anchorage provided.

Of course, *Grand Cru* has always known her place as the ideal retreat for just them. Whether just the two of them on a sail, or just enough alone time after the kids' bedtime, the perfect date night could be just lying on deck, watching the stars go by. Scott and Heidi found the perfect recipe for their time onboard, sometimes simply talking, listening, and enjoying the magic that happens by just being together, with just a little water and sky mixed in.

As they stood before their boat and sipped their coffee, they watched the soaking manatee enjoy a shower from the water stream of the onboard AC through-hull. Their guests would arrive shortly, and the workday would begin. *Of course, it isn't really working if you are doing what you truly enjoy,* Scott thought. Maybe they should come up with a new name for that kind of work. There could be some kind of code word used so that everyone using it knows and recognizes the others using it, and they can all just wink and smile! He grinned as he imagined this play out in his head.

"You know, eighteen years ago, we were enjoying our morning coffee together, watching that beautiful Hawaiian landscape from our balcony," she said. "Can you believe it's been that long? I can close my eyes, and it seems like just yesterday I was coasting down that mountaintop on a bike."

"Time flies when you're having fun," Scott said as he took another sip. They stared at each other one-second longer than just a stare as he touched her hand and played with the ring on her finger. "Well, you had to say yes, didn't you? It was a long way to the bottom!"

"Well, we certainly got a lot of momentum going downhill! You know, Scott, when you think of all the years we've worked together as a team, who would have known that it would lead to something so satisfying as helping others accomplish the same thing? Do you remember when we started thinking about doing this? Remember how people were always asking us, 'How do you do it, working together all day and still enjoying being together at the end of the day?'"

"Well, think about it," said Scott. "We started seeing some really good friends lose their businesses, and we've seen some really great couples end their relationships. I guess we just figured, you know . . . it just didn't have to happen."

"Exactly," Heidi answered. "And it looks like our new couple is heading our way. Ready to take them on the downhill ride of their lives?" She laughed and went to greet their new guests.

Meet Mark and Melissa

Heidi walked up to Mark and Melissa as they approached the boat, watching them as both of their eyes followed the mast to the top.

"Welcome. We're excited to have both of you aboard today. It looks like we have great weather for a perfect day on the water."

"Well, it's actually the first time on a boat for both of us, so the smoother, the better," answered Melissa. Her look eased from its initial apprehension. Mark replied, "You know, I've always wanted to try sailing. Thought it would be great to just cast the ropes and head south somewhere."

"It's lines, actually. Ropes are on land, but on a boat, we call them lines. We haven't even left the dock, and already a lesson shared," said Scott as he came over to shake hands. "So what do you say we go ahead and cast these lines and head out?" He took their bags and headed over to the lifelines to help them aboard. "Have a seat, and we'll be under way in just a sec."

As the couple boarded *Grand Cru*, a day of serendipity began. Mark and Melissa were drawn to this experience because they were struggling to find the balance in their own lives. They were trying to fit together all of their pieces. Frustrated with their situation, they felt that there was a way to connect everything together, there was a solution, and they just needed to take the first step. As they came aboard, they felt their journey beginning, and they imagined the possibilities that awaited them.

Scott and Heidi cast off the dock lines and eased away from the slip, throttling forward gently into the open water. Things do happen for a reason, don't they? Scott glanced at their new crew as he announced, "Let the journey begin!"

Chapter 3

THE COUPLECEO

Two are better than one, because they have a good return for their labor: If either of them falls down, one can help the other up. But pity anyone who falls and has no one to help them up. Also, if two lie down together, they will keep warm. But how can one keep warm alone? Though one may be overpowered, two can defend themselves. A cord of three strands is not quickly broken.

—Ecclesiastes 4:9-12

G*rand Cru* left the red markers to port as she channeled out from the marina. The low hum of the diesel engine provided the undertone to the conversation. "Welcome aboard," said Scott. "Heidi and I are thrilled that you could join

11

us today. We are really looking forward to our day together with you. We know it must be hard to get away from everything for a while, but we know you'll leave with some good takeaways from our time afloat."

"Yes, it really is tough to extract ourselves from the store, but both of us agreed that it was the right thing to do," said Melissa. "We know everything isn't exactly where it needs to be, but we both are determined to find a way to get there, right, honey?"

"It's good to get out, I agree," Mark nodded as he inhaled the fresh air.

"We look at this like sailing," Scott explained. "We sail a course, experience things along the way, and just teach what we've figured out along the journey. We're not licensed therapists or anything like that. Truth be told, we've never even been to a therapist. We just like sharing what we've learned, both from our own experience and from working with other successful CoupleCEOs.

"But many people have told us that we seem to have it figured out. We successfully run our business ventures, we have three happy, healthy sons, and at the end of each day, we hold hands, look each other in the eye, and say, 'I love you.' So not sure that we've figured everything out, but today we plan to share stories and philosophies, building a framework that you can apply to your business and your relationship. Sound like a plan?"

"Definitely," replied Mark. "We're excited to learn."

"Scott and I work in a very interactive way," said Heidi, "feeding each other with ideas, questions, and mutual discussion. So we want the dialogue with both of you to also be very interactive, a process of drawing on your questions, your concerns, your fears, as well as your hopes. We want to know what keeps you up at night, what desires you have that need to be fulfilled, what frustrations you encounter, and where you ultimately want to be. We also want to know what's working well, what attracted you to each other, and what motivates you to run your business. We want to layer into that what we have experienced and learned along the way, and provide some solutions that we hope will help you develop and implement your new personal strategies.

The Foundational Building Blocks for the CoupleCEO

"You see, our framework delves into what we call the Five Fundamental Pieces of the Puzzle. We believe they represent the Foundational Building Blocks for the CoupleCEO to realize a complete life where all the pieces fit together. We explore and examine these five components:

CoupleCEO
FRAMEWORK

CoupleCEO Framework

Intimacy | Time Management | Health & Fitness | Business Strategies | Goals & Dreams

- Time management
- Business strategies
- Health and fitness
- Intimacy
- Goals and dreams

"We find that these five areas of focus for the couples we work with represent vastly different parts of their life, but coupled together," Heidi continued, "they provide you with various dimensions to your relationship, allowing it to grow stronger and develop deeper roots over time."

"And by building a complete lifestyle of shared goals and dreams," Scott added, "your business can become a platform to realize and enjoy a life together, from sunrise to sunset and beyond!"

There was a brief moment of silence as the four of them sat in the cockpit. Mark and Melissa glanced at each other with an anticipation of both anxiety and trepidation. As they shifted in their seat cushions, there was a nervous energy as they realized they were not merely audience members taking notes, but engaged participants. Like undressing in a roomful of strangers, they soon would realize that everyone looked pretty much like everyone else when you reveal what's underneath, when you share your concerns and your fears and your hopes. They say the truth shall set you free, but freedom has its price and its reward. The naked truth is no place for modesty. Mark and Melissa came here for solutions and strategies, and with everything on the line, they would do what it takes to find their answers.

Two Strengths Are Better Than One

"We've heard you use this expression 'CoupleCEO.' What does it mean to you?" Melissa said. "I hadn't heard it before finding out about you."

"We coined the term 'CoupleCEO' because we understand that a couple running a business together is very different from a business being managed and owned by one person with all other workers as employees," Heidi explained. "What we've found to be interesting is that when this term is shared with individual business owners, they get a funny look on their faces as though they don't get it. But when we would talk to couples who run their businesses together and use the term 'CoupleCEO,' the term seemed to resonate immediately. I like to get a little literal in our description."

Heidi began to describe it in greater detail. "When most people consider the definition of the word 'couple,' they think of two, a pair. According to both dictionary.com and Merriam-Webster.com, this is the first definition. But if you look further into some of the additional definitions, you find 'two equal and opposite forces that act along parallel lines.' This is the definition that resonates with us in our explanation of the term 'CoupleCEO.' Let's break it down:

"'Two equal'—This is a very important reality when a couple come together to run a business. They need to understand and respect that this is your mantra—you are two people working equally to make your business successful. It does not matter if he is the doctor and she is the office manager. The equal goal is to make the business a success. He has to administer the best care and earn referrals for the business to succeed. She needs to make the appointment and payment processes customer-friendly so the customer is happy and they get referrals. If these are not considered equal, then the equilibrium is off, and there is no balance.

"'Opposite forces'—The best couples have opposite, but complementing, strengths. Our favorite metaphor is that of mowing the lawn. Each of you is capable of pushing the mower, but if you push it together, you are wasting energy. You will be most productive if one pushes and the other bags the clippings. The tasks are equally important for the job to get done efficiently. Determining strengths and weaknesses should happen at the onset of deciding to run a business together. If you wait until you're down the road and try to push the mower together, many details will get lost, and it will lead to disaster.

"'Act along parallel lines'—As a couple, you are working side by side on the same road to success. The two in the CoupleCEO are working in concert together and at the same pace. You each have the same goal of the company achieving success, and you should be hand in hand in parallel motion to achieve that success. If you aren't parallel, you are not in balance."

Mark chimed in, "You mean like two people working as the head of the company is better than one?"

"Exactly," replied Scott. "There's nothing better than a couple working in concert together to advance their company and their life forward. Two is always better than one. The old adage 'Two heads are better than one' is certainly true. The uniqueness with a CoupleCEO is that each person has an equally vested interest in the success of the company as well as sharing their lives together. Employees can be loyal and might even have profit sharing to keep them more motivated about the success. But it is not their company; they did not start this company from the ground up. And even if there is a business partner in a business, the focus is merely the success of just the business. But as a CoupleCEO, the motivations are equal, and the division of duties can ebb and flow as needed. Neither partner has an *employee* mentality. You are sharing a business and a life together."

"We can totally identify with that," said Melissa. "I've been involved with our family business since I was a young girl, but when Mark and I found ourselves running it ourselves years later, we shared the same ups and downs that I saw my parents go through. We owned our own destiny with where we were taking the business, but the business was steering our lives down a path."

"You were letting the business manage you and your life, rather than you and your life managing your business. It's like you found yourselves on a boat, which was your business," said Scott, "which was taking your life in a certain direction. You weren't steering it where you wanted to go, but the winds were taking you somewhere else. You see, the nice thing about sailing is that you can tack your way to where you want to be, no matter where the winds are blowing. The wind doesn't force your direction; it merely provides the momentum to get there. You need to be able to steer your way to where you want to be."

"Always the sailing metaphor, Scott," said Heidi. "But I think you see the point he's making, don't you?"

"Yes, we do," chimed both Mark and Melissa together.

"We owned a restaurant at one time, and we both would do whatever was needed to get through our evenings," Heidi said. "A server might not put on a fresh roll of toilet paper in the bathroom because it is not their 'job.' As part of a CoupleCEO, you both do whatever is needed. It is very similar to your home; you run your household together. You each may have tasks and roles that you manage. For example, one of you might do most of the inside duties, and the other, the outside. One might do the bills, while the other might do the dishes. But the goal is to run a happy, successful home where all of the tasks are completed, and friends and family enjoy spending time with you. We like the term 'CoupleCEO' because it's the same philosophy in running your business. One of the added benefits is that a CoupleCEO always has two perspectives to situations instead of one.

"For example, during one of the economic downturns, it was necessary to lay off some of our employees. This is never an easy task. If Scott had been running the company alone, he would have handled it in a much more abrupt manner. We talked it through at length and established a staged approach that worked better for our employees as well as working toward our necessary goal of decreasing overhead. Two heads provided the perspective and the balance to handle a very difficult situation with ease and poise."

"Think of the expression 'Two strengths are better than one,'" Heidi continued. "One of our case studies is of a successful CoupleCEO who own a magazine. Their strengths independently are impressive, but when combined, they are truly amazing. They began their company with a hired manager working with Margaret. After less than a year, Margaret called Aaron and said, 'We need to fire this manager, and you need to come work here with me.' Within a year, the magazine became

TWO HEADS ARE BETTER THAN ONE

profitable and the leader in its niche market, and still is twenty-six years later. They clearly were much more productive running their company together. But when asked what was their most challenging time in the business, it was when they were not managing their magazine together. They have more balance when running their business together."

"But with our store, it seems as though we are constantly stepping over each other, getting in each other's way, like there's no plan of attack for who should do what," Melissa said. "We have constant arguments over getting inventory done, handling purchasing issues, dealing with customer complaints, not to mention finding new ways to attract customers. There is no organization as to who does what. I'm not a perfectionist, but I want to at least finish one thing before jumping to the next. In our business, there are variables that are constant every day, like hours of operation, but many unknowns too, like when a blizzard comes through, and no customers come through our doors for several days."

Mark said, "I guess I'm the one who really bounces around from one thing to the next because there's just so much that has to be done. I can see the big picture, but meanwhile, all of the 'stuff' still needs to be completed."

"Our magazine couple is an example," Heidi pointed out. "They have different strengths and expertise that make the magazine a success—he is the writer, and she is the editor. He might find the advertisers, but she closes them. She shared an interesting and entertaining story about going on a sales call together. Aaron hates to sell ads, but Margaret taught him the method, and then they went on a call together, and he took the lead. He totally botched it. They were almost at yes, but rather than close the deal, he got them to where they said no to a free ad. They learned each other's fortes and flaws.

"Another couple shared that he starts projects, and she finishes them. At first, this was a problem for them. He would get angry that she would 'take over,' and she thought he was lazy for not finishing. But when they removed the emotions and the personal attacks, and looked at it from a business standpoint, they realized this could be an advantage. He is the thinker and the visionary, and she is the logistical implementer. When you put these together, it can be incredibly effective. So now, they understand that he will take tasks anywhere from 15 to 85 percent, and she sees them through to completion."

Know Your Type

Heidi went on to explain that it is extremely important that a CoupleCEO have a clear outline of their strengths and weaknesses. In the early stages of the company growth (when it's just the two of them working from home), they have to share the load with just the two of them, so they need to know who is best at what responsibilities.

"This is not an exercise to be taken lightly in a brief conversation over coffee," Heidi warned. "This should be written down with job titles and job descriptions since you are essentially building the entire organization, virtually, and creating your organizational chart, complete with everyone's duties and responsibilities to refer to."

Scott asked Melissa, "Do you have an organizational chart for your business?"

Melissa replied, "No, but neither did my parents. You just do what has to get done. When I started working in the store as a kid, I wasn't given a specific job or title. If the floors needed to be swept, or shelves needed to be stocked, I just did it."

"Having an organizational map in place is important for the longevity of the business," explained Heidi. "You told us earlier that you don't have any plan in place for who should do what. If this was written down, then it is real, and it also helps for your employees to understand their responsibilities. As you build this organizational chart with responsibilities, you are probably going to quickly see that there are tasks and jobs that should be getting done but aren't because it was never written down."

Scott described how one of the underlying concepts of the CoupleCEO framework is the understanding of personality typing. "Clearly identifying your own personality type, your partner's type, as well as that of those around your work and personal life will be a powerful and significant tool in understanding, communicating with, and working more successfully with those around you. Personality typing explores what motivates people and influences their behavior. It is important to understand that everyone has inborn, natural preferences that can be identified as key characteristics of personality.

"I'm a certified MBTI® Practitioner, meaning that we administer the Myers-Briggs Type Indicator (MBTI)® Instrument for our clients to help them determine their preferences," Scott said. "As the most widely used personality assessment tool in the world, it's a wonderful tool to begin the process of understanding personality types. By utilizing this as a foundational tool to build upon, you, as a couple, can understand personality type differences and similarities, which can help you build a stronger and more cohesive team as a CoupleCEO, both now as well as into the future.

"I want you to try something. Each of you, write your name down using your opposite hand, the hand you don't normally write with. How did you do? It is a lot harder than using your other hand, isn't it? Think of your personality type the same way. There is a natural preference that is your inborn tendency. The sooner you can identify those preferences, the sooner you can learn to explore the potential that is really you. As a couple, understanding each person's type can help develop the strategies to effectively succeed together as a team. One person's preference can complement another's opposites. Or both of you can have similar preferences in areas and be careful to not step over each other."

PERSONALITY TYPE WHEEL

*Note: We have developed a descriptive summary of each spoke of the Personality Type Wheel, which can be found in the Appendix.

Scott explained that there are four dichotomies that everyone's preferences fall into. Each of the four dichotomies is made up of a pair of opposite preferences, which means that there are eight preferences. When these preferences are combined in all possible ways, they form sixteen distinct personality types. Couples can identify their individual types and learn how their behavior and others' can be consistent based on the differences in how each of us uses our type through the perception and judgment in our daily interactions.

"Think about the importance of the type in building and sustaining your organization. Additionally, the type can be an important tool in working effectively as a CoupleCEO in all aspects of our lives. Does your partner perceive information literally, or [does he or she] interpret and add meaning? Does your partner get energized with roomfuls of people, or in secluded spaces by [himself or herself]? Does your partner like to get decisions made, or [does he or she] like to delay decisions until more information arrives? [Does he or she] deal with things logically, or emotionally? Does your partner like to make decisions? How does your partner get energized?

"You can begin to appreciate how a clear understanding of the type will improve how your relationship works, your business works, and every aspect of your life, really. For example, as an entrepreneur, you can clearly identify everything that needs to be performed in every aspect of the company. From producing the goods or services, to managing the eventual staff, to handling the finances, to attracting and then selling to the customers or clients, to even building the websites, there is a job description for all of it."

"Of course," Heidi said, "you won't have employees to fill out every job title that is created. You'll be wearing most of those job titles yourself initially. But remember that with the beauty of the CoupleCEO business model, there are two of you to wear hats. But make sure you don't wear the same hat."

"Remember that you'll figure out who's better at one job or another," Scott added. "This is where the type plays an important role. Why perform a job that is like writing with your wrong hand? You won't be happy at it, and you probably will not perform it as well as the job suiting your preferences. And you'll know what jobs you mutually share a weakness in, and those positions are the first ones you fill. Filling those positions with individuals best suited for the work will create a strong foundation for your business."

As the discussion continued, both Melissa and Mark realized that they had never really taken that hard assessment of themselves. By understanding that as a couple, one's weakness may be the other's strength, and by recognizing this, they could position their collective strengths to allow them to accomplish amazing things. They were beginning to comprehend that they would need to spend time analyzing both their personal and professional assessments in order to fully identify their own preferences.

"Let's take a moment and have you write a few things down on paper," Heidi began as she gave Mark and Melissa paper and pens. "First, let's begin by writing down your five strengths and weaknesses. Then write down your spouse's five strengths and weaknesses. But understand that it's okay to have these weaknesses. It's just like writing with your 'wrong' hand. You'd just prefer not to do it." She gave them a few moments to write. Melissa was done quickly; Mark needed a bit more time.

They were surprised as they shared their answers. They both agreed that one of Mark's strengths was his knowledge of their online store and his ability to attract their nontraditional customers, but they also admitted that Melissa had not encouraged that change in their business. A weakness of hers that they both wrote down was that she is content running the business the way her parents did. She is adverse to change. Now that she has admitted her weakness and knows that Mark has a strength of adapting to change, his strength could really lead to some new successes for their business, if she supports the change to attracting customers outside of the store.

"We will have a few more of these breakthroughs as the day progresses," Heidi said, "but we haven't finished explaining why we use the term 'CoupleCEO' and why it is such a basic concept for couples running their business together to understand."

Share the Highs and the Lows

"Melissa, remember when you were a kid in elementary school, and you gave your first speech in front of the class, how the kids applauded and your teacher told you, 'Great job'?" Scott asked. "You just couldn't wait to get home and tell your mom or dad all about it, right?"

"Sure, I would run to the store to tell Dad," said Melissa. "I was always so excited to share my day with him. I remember doing my afternoon chores at the store and wondering if there was anything I had forgotten to share with him that day."

Her eyes filled with tears as she remembered her departed father. "He died so young, really. Only sixty-eight. I think this store, his business, and his passion, took too much out of him.

Never really found the time to do the other things he liked to do. Fly-fishing. He did like fly-fishing. Only he never seemed to get out from the store enough to do it as frequently as he wanted."

Heidi continued, "Melissa, that same excitement to share your wins, that same joy you experienced as a child, that excitement permeates with CoupleCEOs, both with big wins and little wins in their company. As a child, your parents are vested in your success. As a CoupleCEO, each partner is vested in each other's success, in his or her shared business and personal success. Being able to connect with each other on all facets of your life is very special."

Scott recalled, "There was a brief period of time, two and a half years, that we did not work together. The world of real estate and home-building was going through a pretty rough spell."

"Scott, it was the worst housing depression this country has ever seen, come on!" Heidi insisted.

"Yes, it was pretty bad," Scott agreed. "Not a fun time in Florida, that's for sure. Heidi had been volunteering for about ten years with a local children's museum, serving for a period as their chairwoman. They had asked her to come onboard the staff as the VP to raise money and help to get the new building developed. It was a huge undertaking, but we agreed that this unique opportunity for the community was worth the time working apart."

"I was physically working seventy hours a week up to opening," Heidi said. "And mentally much more—this opening was all-consuming. The week after the opening, I was in the kitchen, and I glanced at Scott and could see that he was carrying a huge burden in our business, without sharing the daily highs and lows with his partner. I had been so consumed by my job that I realized I hadn't checked in with Scott about our businesses. I was devastated that I had allowed myself to disconnect from my partner."

"So Heidi and I made an impromptu date night," Scott said. "Over dinner, I explained to her just how grave our financial situation was with the business. I had been working with the bank and coming to decisions on my own."

"I knew then that I didn't want that to ever happen again," Heidi shared. "We had shared the joys of the boom times working and traveling together. We took some of our best vacations while the market was soaring. The overwhelming guilt I felt that he had to manage the lows alone is hard to convey in words. We knew then that this time working apart would be short-lived. We knew that we would get through those down times together and we would work together as we built back up to enjoy the good times together again."

She paused before continuing because she knew that this was strongly resonating with them. "Remember, CoupleCEOs work together in concert to build their company through ups and downs. They share duties and understand each other's strengths and weaknesses. They relish the good times together and rally from the down times hand-in-hand. CoupleCEOs are strongest because they are a couple first, working in tandem as a CEO. This way of approaching their business is what gives them balance.

"So, have we adequately answered your question about what a CoupleCEO is?" asked Heidi.

Mark and Melissa answered in tandem, "We definitely get it."

Scott and Heidi were pleased to know that Mark and Melissa understood the significance of the term "CoupleCEO." With the seed planted, the foundation had been set to begin delving into the details of how Mark and Melissa could create their more balanced lifestyle.

Chapter 4

THE BALANCE GO-ROUND

Life is like riding a bicycle. To keep balance, you must keep moving.

—Albert Einstein

Mark began, "You speak of balance a lot, but the hardest thing we struggle with in finding balance is juggling all of the commitments. Work needs us; my parents and even our adult kids need us. I am so busy tending to everyone else's needs—how can I possibly find balance for me?"

Heidi responded, "Let's call this idea 'The Balance Go-Round'—How do we find the balance between family and work?

The Balance-Go-Round

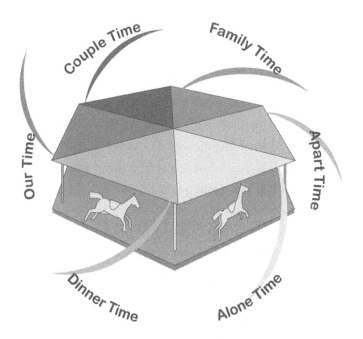

"You know, it's interesting because this question is so often the first concern of a couple *considering* working together. It is also the most frequent *struggle* of a couple who have been working together. We have found that the best advice we can give is to create distinct *times* that create boundaries. Understand that family has needs that are separate from the business needs, and if either is ignored, the outcome can be devastating.

Apart Time, Family Time, and Our Time "We're going to make the assumption that you make *work* time. The work time may not be efficient or well-run, and we deal with that separately, but you get out of bed every day and go to work. For you two it's to your store, but for others it could be at a home office or a manufacturing plant. Wherever it is, you make work time. But the question is, do you make *apart* time, *family* time, and *our* time?"

"We've discovered that the happiest and most productive couples create times to satisfy their various needs," Scott added. "A CoupleCEO that we worked with are attorneys and met in college. One of their favorite *our time* activities is to attend the football games of their alma mater. Another CoupleCEO that runs a chiropractic practice makes *apart time*, he with his paintball team, and she caring for her mother."

"We consistently find that with the majority of the CoupleCEOs we work with, making distinct times for themselves, separately as well as together, outside of their work was important for happiness and achieving their balance," Heidi said.

"So you're saying that I need to carve out the time? But how?" Mark asked. "My father recently broke his hip, and my mom's dementia has been getting steadily worse over the last eighteen months. I know I need to spend some time with them and get my arms around the situation, but how do I find the time?"

"You should specifically 'chunk your responsibilities' into manageable time periods and allocate specific schedules to each area that needs addressing," Scott explained. "This term was first used by Tony Robbins, and we know it works well. If you need to chunk some time for your parents, do it. Just realize that it can't be a fully consuming effort that detracts from everything else. Spend some time on it, chunk it, and you can go back to it later for more. The point is that you can touch a lot of areas in need of attention, but don't have a tunnel vision approach that forgets about everything else. You can go back to each issue when you address that activity chunk.

"Think of it like reading a collection of books. You allocate a chunk of time for the first book, place a bookmark to keep your spot, close the book, and move on to the next one. Just like reading a collection of books, one chapter at a time, we organize the activities of our lives—a couple of pages at a time. The more you chip away at something, you'll discover that eventually you've finished the entire book."

"And remember to make *apart time,*" Heidi added. "You sleep together, eat breakfast together, work together, have dinner together, but each of you is an individual, and that needs to be recognized, so create *apart time.* Don't schedule it like a dentist appointment; let it come naturally—but commit to it. You love your partner, those dreamy blue eyes, etc., but give it a break and separate. Don't smother each other."

"That's right," agreed Scott. "We really enjoy walking and jogging together—it is part of our commitment to our healthy lifestyle. But we are committed to occasionally driving to Bayshore Boulevard (our favorite walk/jog spot), and we head in opposite directions. We are a bit competitive, so we see who gets back first. But also, our minds are clearer when we reunite, and we often have new ideas that we are anxious to share."

"Our boat is truly a family boat. Even the name is indicative," said Heidi. "But it is Scott's haven. He loves to accomplish boat tasks. He can spend all day on *Grand Cru*, doing tasks that the rest of us see as mundane and monotonous, but he disembarks feeling completely satisfied. So although traveling on the boat is family time, preparing the boat is his favorite *apart time*.

"Melissa, do you have a favorite activity?"

"I used to go to yoga on Sundays, but now we go see Mark's parents on Sundays, so I haven't been in about six months," Melissa explained.

"Melissa, I don't know about where *you* live, but here there are yoga classes on days other than Sunday," Heidi chastised. "Make another time. Don't ignore who you are and what makes you happy. If you do, you will end up resenting Mark and his parents. And I know you don't want to feel that way about your in-laws.

"And another tip is, don't always lunch together! Scott used to eat lunch with his old business partner every day. So when we started working together, you should have seen his big blue, puppy dog eyes when I said I'm not available for lunch."

"She's right," said Scott. "In fact, an added benefit to not eating lunch together every day has been that I have been able to make time to lunch with my father. I value the time I spend with him, and even gain great perspective on business and life topics over our lunchtime meals."

"When my girlfriends began a lunch group, Lunch Bunch, and invited me," Heidi continued, "I thought, *I don't have time to go have a leisurely lunch with my girlfriends; I have a business to run.* Let me tell you that the therapy I receive from time with my Lunch Bunch girls is priceless. My Lunch Bunch is my favorite *apart time*."

Scott and Heidi continued to provide different stories and ideas to Mark and Melissa. They described that you don't need special plans for lunch every day because sometimes just quietly sitting at your desk and finishing a book or reading a magazine can be a well-deserved respite to your day. But, they instructed, if you do have lunch together, make it a business lunch, make it productive—plus, then you get to write it off and not feel guilty.

They admitted that many of the CoupleCEOs they've worked with lunch together. They found this especially true in an office environment that did not allow for much interaction throughout the day, such as a doctor's office with one seeing patients and the other managing the front office. They found their time together at lunch was necessary to keep each other filled in on the daily happenings. An added benefit of this was that it reduced the need for business discussion to continue after going home in the evening.

"Sometimes CoupleCEOs tell us, 'But our kids are grown and out of the house. They don't live near us, so we don't need family time,'" Heidi explained. "But what we explain in the lesson on 'Making Family Time' is that family time has different meanings for everyone."

The lesson on family time continued as Heidi detailed the various types of family time that can be created. She reminded Mark and Melissa that even though their kids were grown up and out of the house, going through some of these examples might stimulate further discussion and ideas that would resonate with them.

Heidi spoke about families with their kids still at home. She pointed out how easy it is in today's technology-consumed world to get sucked into the entire family just watching TV or staring at handheld devices.

"Just look at the childhood obesity rate," said Scott. "You know, we could do an entire series on this subject; it is so maddening to Heidi and me."

"Agreed," Heidi replied. "But family time must be planned. And that includes you both as well, you empty nesters. Don't sit back and expect quality time together to just magically happen.

"There are too many distractions in family life today—technology distractions, friend distractions, and even extracurricular activities. The whole family going to watch Johnny play soccer cannot be your only family time. We tell the parents, 'Be the parent—your kids are not likely going to say, "Can we please go to the art festival or the opera?"' When you are committed to family time, it should be filled with new adventures and experiences for the entire family."

"We know of couples who only go out with and travel with their friends. They never go out with just themselves or their family. Part of the aspect of spending time together is to connect, just the two of you, away from friends and family. And it doesn't have to cost a lot of money. Art festivals are free. Our local newspaper printed a picture of our middle son, Seth, on Scott's shoulders at an art festival when he was about three years old. It is mounted and on prominent display in Scott's office among many of his awards. It is a constant reminder that among all of the accomplishments taking place at work, family is in the center."

"That's right," Scott said. "Farmer's markets are free. Just check out your local paper or the paper's website for free and cheap things to do on the weekends. Typically, it will list such things as farmer's markets, free concerts, and so on. We tell folks to get active outside, and if they have kids, to get active with their kids. There are so many things to do, from going on bike rides, to playing dodge ball or ultimate Frisbee, to throwing the baseball. Rake the leaves, and let them jump on the piles. Make water balloons and toss them. Yes, we have boys, so our activities tend to be very physical and often competitive, but you get the idea—go outside, and get physical with your kids.

"Just take walks together. It's highly underrated."

Heidi laughed, "Definitely. Scott and I love our walks together."

"Melissa, remember those bike rides we used to take?" Mark said. "Those were great for getting a little workout, and I remember how we cooled off afterward."

Melissa looked at him and smiled.

"But the weather sucks where we live, Scott," complained Melissa. "We can't go out for six months of the year."

"Okay, we're from Florida," defended Scott. "And, of course, everyone should be from Florida, but there are some great non-outdoor activities for your family time, such as family game night. But make sure each person in the house gets to pick; otherwise, the youngest will have you playing *Candy Land* until you want to torch the game board."

"Every year at the holidays, the gift our family looked forward to opening most was the new game we added," Heidi said. "Also, TV night, only *one* night per week, was always popular, and we'd always pick an interactive show. Be sure to pick a show that everyone agrees to watch together. We are not reality TV show folks, but *The Voice, American Idol,* and *America's Got Talent* have always been good options to keep a dialogue going after each performance.

"Our youngest son, Adam, liked the show *Brain Games* because it was very interactive and educational too. You know, another fun activity is playing charades—this will always be sure to garner the most laughs, but we always included some harder categories, such as books, characters, and famous people, that served as teaching moments."

"You know, honey, you can't forget our famous card games," said Scott.

"Of course, I don't know how famous they are," responded Heidi. "But Scott and I have a running game of gin rummy that we play when we're unwinding and just settling into family time mode. I'm sure that you'll see us at ninety still shuffling the deck for another hand."

"Mark, you mentioned your parents are having health issues," Scott said. "With aging parents, either living with you or not, find meaningful activities to do with them. They can't move at the pace you do, and their minds may not be as sharp, but make a day or night each week that is dedicated to being with them.

"If you have other family in town, have everyone over for dinner. The stories they will share, even if repeated, are great for other generations to hear. If they are still mobile, go for a walk in the park, and take in a concert, if your town offers that."

"Play cards or mah-jongg," Heidi added, "or whatever they enjoy that keeps their mind thinking. Go to a museum, or go to a pottery studio. If they are still mobile, try yoga."

They waited to let this sink in with both Mark and Melissa. They knew they were giving them a lot to digest, but they knew how important it was to share these nuggets with them.

"With your kids out of the house, grown up, now it's just the two of you," began Heidi. "You must remember to still cherish and preserve your *our time*, and not take that time for granted."

"You would think this would be the easiest, right?" said Scott. "Spending time together is not just eating a meal, but really tasting all of the flavors and textures of the food the way a real foodie would enjoy it."

"Exactly," echoed Heidi. "Great metaphor, Scott. You really are the king of metaphors."

"Well, I think it just describes what I'm trying to say. If the balance is lost, it's most often because *our time* is not part of the routine. You have to savor the moments as a couple. Remember the excitement that occurred when you were dating, ages ago? Discovering new things about each other and experiencing new things together? Bring those new experiences and excitement into what you're doing today. For example, our kids would go away to camp for seven weeks over the summer, and prior to their departure, we might find ourselves in a rut. We needed some disruption from the normal activities."

"So what did we do?" Heidi said. "We would get giddy just before they went away for a few reasons, such as we didn't have to do the car pool every day and night, we could eat at any time, anywhere in the house, we could take a skinny-dip in the pool, we could spend our Saturdays doing what we wanted rather than what the kids' schedules dictated.

"But we would also say, 'Well, now we can work as late as we want every day.' Don't get stuck in that rut; you still need to make *our time.*"

They could see that Mark and Melissa slowly understood the message, but they still seemed trapped in the dilemma of where to begin. "Okay, so how do we make *our time?*" questioned Melissa. "Our business seems to consume us; we have to live, eat, and breathe it in order for it to succeed."

"Okay," Heidi responded. "Here are three incredibly simple *our time* ideas that you can incorporate immediately. Let's break these down:

1. **Have a date night.** Do this one night a week, just for the two of you, with no business talk. Go to a movie, go for a long walk, listen to music in the park, and just make time for the two of you to do something that you both enjoy. If you are on a tight budget because all of your resources have been put into your business, don't let that stop you. You don't have to go out to eat at a fancy restaurant; instead, pack a picnic, and go sit in a park. Our favorite date nights would be just sitting on our boat, listening to the water and watching the stars. As one of the CoupleCEOs we interviewed told us, 'We would drop suggestive hints during the week about date night, building up the momentum.' It can become the romantic highlight of your week.

2. **Play cards together.** It is a very simple activity that is just for the two of you, and to make it fun, keep a running tally of the winner and loser. As we've mentioned, Scott

and I do this on a regular basis. Up until my grandmother passed away after fifty years of marriage, she was very pleased that she was the winner of their ongoing gin rummy game. But if you prefer backgammon or mahjongg, that's fine. The point is to decide today what that will be, and start playing.

3. **Honor the most important golden rule: no business talk at the dinner table!** It is difficult for a business owner to ever turn off thinking, sweating, and talking about his or her business. You see a duck crossing the road, and it reminds you that you forgot to send your customer, Mr. Waddle, his replacement part for his widget. And even if everyone in your family (this could be you and your spouse, or could include every member of your family) works in the business, dinnertime should be to discuss non-business topics, to take a break."

"That's right, Heidi," said Scott. "You know, we seem to have some of the liveliest dinner conversations. When our son's friends would come for dinner, they often were amazed at the amount of candor during dinner. All men plus the mom equals many of the discussion topics are not appropriate to repeat (penises, farts, and other bodily functions). Even if no kids or other adults are living with you, you can still stick to the rule of *no* business talk."

"Scott and I had date night for the first ten years of our marriage," said Heidi. "And the only time we ever discussed business was if there was a crisis, and, of course, there were a few. But even during those times, such as when we were in the midst of discussing the stark realities of the 2007 housing crash, date night was the time for a very emotional dialogue, complete with tears and baring our souls about what financial disaster would mean to us. So it wasn't a business discussion about finding resolution to these issues; it was about sharing our feelings and connecting our emotions." Scott and Heidi connected with each other with a shared glance, both remembering those talks that extended well into the evening.

Mark interrupted their thoughts. "It just seems that for the past three years, since we took over the business without her parents, we haven't discussed anything other than the business and, of course, the new struggles of helping to care for my parents. So I'm really not sure just where to start."

"The best way to start is by beginning immediately with a plan," answered Heidi. "And just take it one step at a time:

1. **Each of you, schedule lunch with a friend this week.** You will return from lunch relaxed and ready for your afternoon.

2. **Schedule date night with the two of you for this weekend.** You will look into each other's eyes on your date night and remember how much fun you had together when you were younger and why you fell in love with each other.

3. **Commit to 'no business talk' at dinner, immediately!** You will enjoy dinnertime in a whole new light, talking with each other about topics you've never discussed before, sharing opinions and learning new perspectives you've never thought of, and just enjoying an entire new dimension to your relationship.

"These first steps begin building the foundation of a balanced relationship."

The Yin-Yang Effect

"Here's the way I look at it," began Scott. "Balance is really just the natural rule of nature—a state of equilibrium in the universe that *must* eventually be realized. It just puts everything back in place. Life must have a certain level of chaos in order to create. We need to have disruptive activity and thought to produce the creativity, build new things, think of new ideas, and grow as individuals, as couples, and even in our businesses. But a sense of balance is what brings it back in order at the end of the day. Your relationship should become like that balance pole you hold as you walk life's tightrope."

Melissa said, "When people say, 'You guys really balance each other,' what does that really mean, Scott?"

"Think of balance like the benefits to our bodies as we strengthen our core muscles," Scott said. "Building up our core strengthens us to perform everyday tasks, such as bending to put on shoes or sitting in a chair, even basic activities of daily living, such as bathing or dressing. It aids in maintaining a healthy back, performing on-the-job tasks, and playing your favorite sport, whether that's golf, tennis, running, or swimming. An added benefit is that strengthening your core can definitely benefit you in sexual activities.

"So balance is like all of those core muscles working together. Like the concept of yin-yang, seemingly contrary forces are interconnected and interdependent—and actually complementary. Opposites are necessary to ensure balance. The yin-yang, working together, actually creates the balance that must exist to perform all of the functions you perceive as vital for a healthy and happy lifestyle."

THE YING-YANG EFFECT

"So a relationship is just like your core muscles," Scott continued. "You need to keep strengthening them in order to perform the complexity of things life calls on us to do every day. Sometimes one set of core muscles supports another set of core muscles, and vice versa. It creates the balance we are talking about. It allows the yin-yang effect to happen.

"Stand here in the cockpit, and try balancing on one leg for thirty seconds. You have the added challenge of being on the water. Feel your core muscles working? Feel one side supporting the other side, and then feel the shift happening back to the other side? Your core muscles do an amazing job of allowing that balance to occur because there is a constant give-and-take among the various muscle groups to allow the balance to happen. It happens without thinking because, with practice, it has become instinctual.

The same thing occurs with practice in a relationship. The various muscle groups work together to provide a balance when life is standing on one leg, so to speak. A constant give-and-take occurs without being conscious of it because the muscle memory has solidified with training.

"I think it's important to stay intuitive to your partner's 'muscles'—when to take the load, and when to transfer the load—to keep that balance in place. It involves listening, talking, and sharing. You can begin to accomplish this by creating the different *times* Heidi told you to make part of your daily routine, just like your daily exercise. By staying 'in shape' with these core muscle groups, your relationship can stay balanced and accomplish great things—at work, at home, and everywhere else you want to go.

"Don't worry if you occasionally lose that balance, just like standing on one leg. It happens. Life does get in the way. Remember, we're not flamingos designed to always stand on one leg. But you will find that the more you try and work those core muscles, and the more your muscle memory kicks in without even thinking about it, the more your relationship and your work will thrive because you are carrying the weight of both of you. With your load shared, you'll travel the journey with more distance, with more clarity, with more profitability, and with more passion.

"So, Melissa, when someone says, 'You really balance each other,' the person is saying that your core is so stable in your relationship that it is evident to others. It means that together you're able to withstand whatever life throws at you. It means that your relationship will get you through it."

Scott and Heidi hoped that after that day, Mark and Melissa would begin to strengthen their core. And that people would begin to see them as CoupleCEOs who truly balance each other.

Chapter 5

GOOD TO GREAT

We are what we repeatedly do; excellence, then, is not an act but a habit.

—Aristotle

"So tell us more about your business," prompted Scott. "What makes it great? What are its challenges? What are your dreams about where it can aspire to? We talked earlier about a bit of stagnation. What new concepts are you working on? Where is it heading?"

"Wow, that's a lot of questions," Melissa exclaimed.

"Well, you know, a business is a lot like a person," Scott said. "It has a personality, has established ways of doing things—some good, some not so good. It has aspects in which it really excels and other aspects that need some work. Just like knowing yourself allows you to become all you can be, really knowing your company can allow you to build it to its full potential.

"But also remember that you own a second-generation family business. You need to constantly be building the business if you want it to continue into the next generation. Remember, when we are building a business as entrepreneurs," Scott said, "what we are really doing is building our 'dream home.' Your goal is to build that business the right way."

Build Your Dream Company

The Entrepreneur's Dream Home

"The business that is being constructed is a reflection of the values, tastes, ideals, as well as a statement you want to say to the world—a legacy for what you stand for and what you are passionate about—right?" said Scott. "Just as that architectural landmark will stand on that property corner for a long, long time, so shall your business, if built right, it will stand the test of the market and of time.

"Just like a house requires the proper land use or zoning, your business requires market feasibility in your particular field of product or service. If you can build your concept, and there is a market for it, even if you need to make some unique differences from the normal standards, let's get the dirt cleared and start building that business.

"The first step, of course, is the proper foundation for the business, one that both of you feel comfortable with and mutually agree is a balanced approach and a proper sharing of responsibilities. Maintaining such a level foundation will mean that the balls that invariably get dropped don't roll down from one person's feet to the other's.

"Assessing personality type will determine who will handle the assortment of tools necessary to construct your dream business. Who wields the hammer better? Who's better at ordering the materials? Who's better at keeping count of the costs? And how about the scheduling?

"So building your dream company requires you to construct an organizational chart with everyone necessary to properly run the business. Just like a layout of the rooms in the house, visualizing the organization of the business is an essential blueprint at the beginning of the construction process. Imagine what it would be like to build your dream house without the construction drawings being created at the onset?

"Of course, we realize that you will have rooms/positions designed in your home/organizational chart that can't be filled immediately with the staffing that will occupy your house/ business. From the president, to the vice president of marketing, to the vice president of finance, to the vice president of operations, to the chief operating officer, to the chief information officer, and on and on, the two of you initially may be filling every position in the company yourselves. But you *must* design your company with all of these positions properly constructed and defined as to *exactly* what they do and to whom they report.

"Think of it as rooms being constructed with all of the details built out, such as electrical, plumbing, air conditioning, drywall, insulation, framing, and paint. You just may not have enough in your budget when you move in for the furniture! But fear not because you are building this house to last a long, long time, and having the layout for the furniture is *much* more important than the furniture itself. Furniture is made to be expendable, just as the employees who will eventually 'furnish' these departments will be. Never build your house or your business upon the irreplaceability of either furniture or certain employees. Neither strategy is advisable in building your dream business that works when you need or want to step away from it."

"Exactly," added Heidi. "We've made that mistake before by having employees who were too irreplaceable. You need to make the position irreplaceable, but not the employee. If you have the architecture of the position well-designed, another person will always be able to step into it and continue the designated functions that are required."

"Build your company, like your dream house, with the grandeur and size that you imagine," encouraged Scott. "Don't let limiting beliefs, such as current resources, get in the way of those dreams. Ask yourself how big your business can naturally become. Create your building foundation in a manner that reflects your visions and your 'big picture' dreams of where your business can go."

"Remember that this business is, and always should be, a reflection of both of you," reminded Heidi, "a reflection of you both as individuals, as a couple, as your legacy to being a part of this big world in which we live. It should be constructed to 'house' these beliefs in what every employee does, says, wears, manufactures, and teaches. Remember that like the builder, you're constructing this business not to live in, but to function as a freestanding reflection of what you want to stand at the corner of Main and Main.

"Systems are the key. Constructing detailed systems of everything that occurs, or *should* occur, in your business allows the business to run efficiently each and every time. But more importantly, it runs as a reflection of who you are. This can't happen by osmosis. It has to be documented so that every employee who ever works for you understands the core beliefs that belong to Mark and Melissa.

"Just like the water should run from the faucet, the toilet should flush, the air conditioner should cool, and the roof should insulate, the processes of the business should be constructed to run efficiently," added Scott.

"The sales processes," Heidi began, "should be totally refined and documented so that every and any salesperson, experienced or inexperienced, could follow a script and a procedure for every prospect and every customer.

"The manufacturing processes should be totally refined and documented so that everything that goes into producing that item is consistent and uniform, each and every time.

"All of the words and images and colors and scents of the business—from the sign on the door, to the brochure, to the website, to your recruitment literature, to your packaging—are carefully crafted to create a unique message reflecting *you*. Mark, as you are creating this online presence, it is important that it reflect that storefront; they are both equal reflections of you. And when it is time for a face-lift to these images, make sure they are adjusted across all platforms. If you ever change a color or a font, it must be consistent. If you ever change the greeting your customers hear when they arrive, it needs to be documented in the manual.

"Do you ever wonder why McDonald's does what it does so well?" asked Scott. "Ray Kroc didn't really build a business of making hamburgers; he built a business about consistent processes for *everything* that the company does, from the time a french fry is in the fryer, to the greeting of the order taker, to the "Two-all-beef-patties, special-sauce, lettuce, cheese, pickles, onions-on-a-sesame-seed-bun" Big Mac, each and every time the company makes one, from Tampa, Florida, to Shanghai, China.

"You must consider what information you will need to receive consistently and accurately to provide the proper feedback on your business. Extracting from the day-to-day operations tells you what was sold, when, and by whom; how many prospects were contacted; how many prospects were converted to customers, and by whom; and how many touches they received before purchasing. The feedback becomes your solution on making the process better and better. This feedback *must* be updated on an ongoing basis. I'm sure that the way your customers were approached when your parents ran the business is quite different than it is today."

"You're absolutely right. I grew up behind the counter of the store," said Melissa. "After school, there weren't activities to attend or sports to practice; there were my chores in the store. My friends came to the store to visit me, but my parents didn't follow your advice—we talked business at the dinner, lunch, and breakfast tables. I didn't realize it at the time, but being so much a part of my family business at such a young age made me appreciate even more the joys of a close family. We were together all the time, from taking inventory to stocking shelves, talking to customers, and, of course, sweeping the floors. It was just natural. It was just who we were.

"But the business seemed easier then. The customers just walked in. We had what they needed. We provided great customer service to everyone, and they always came back. It didn't seem like we had to focus on finding our customers, marketing our store, or lowering our margins to get the sale. But competition has just gotten crazy, from the big-box stores to the Internet sites."

"I've been trying to get a foothold online," Mark began. "I'm just a bit overwhelmed trying to figure it all out, and these companies that want to get you set up charge a fortune, and we're concerned about laying out capital right now. So it just seems to make more sense getting it all done yourself, but this is a whole new universe with tons of information overload—you know what I mean?"

Your Business Has a Personality

"Let's step back a second," Scott suggested. "Remember, your business has a personality, right? So let's get to know her a little bit better first. Is your business trying to find customers for your products, or is your business finding products that your customers really want?

"You have to have the tools to really explore the personality of your business. If you look in the proverbial mirror to see who the business really is, you'll be much more effective at finding customers attracted to what you are selling or even creating products that they truly crave.

"So understanding who your customers are *is* really at the core of marketing your business. What really is marketing? Does a typical entrepreneur view it as simply a promotion, advertising, branding, a brochure, a press release, a Facebook page, or a Twitter account? Is it just that catch-all bucket of bells and whistles a business has to gently prod, shove, convince, explain, amaze, and inform all about its offerings to its customers in an attempt to bag yet another sale for the good of the company's revenues?

"What we need to remember is that marketing is the road map that connects your goods and services to your customers' wants," said Scott. "Your customer is the destination to your journey, and just as you need to know where you're going when you depart, you need to know your customer before you begin your trip. If you travel all the way to get to your customer with the wrong thing, that marketing road map has become a wasted road trip. The superhighway is filled with companies and businesses with wasted journeys of unneeded goods, not knowing who their customer was, and therefore never arriving to the land of profits."

"So what you mean is that if you know what your business is really good at doing for your customer, you know what to tell your prospects that would make them interested enough to buy your product?" Melissa asked.

"Yes, but you also would know *which* prospects would be *most* interested in what you are selling. In fact, you wouldn't need prospects; you would just focus on those who are customers. For some of them, it will be their first time buying from you. But they've always been looking for you. You've just made it easier for them to find you," added Scott.

"So it is not only knowing which products are good for your prospects; it also is identifying the best prospects for your products?" Melissa said. "This strategy specifically targets the ability to market online and not just wait for the customers to come through the doors?"

Scott nodded and said: "Online marketing is a tactic to promote your product, but there is a deeper understanding of marketing that many business owners never quite grasp. You need to understand this before you ever tactically market your business or product. When it comes to selling what you make or what you do, it doesn't really matter what *you* want. What you want is unimportant. The only thing that truly matters is what your customer wants. And ironically, what he wants, he may not really know he wants because everything that we purchase, everything that we want to buy, all comes from deep down in our subconscious thoughts. It is only when we send the buying decision back into our conscious reality that we construct a rational argument as to why we should buy the good or service that we really want through fact, reason, and logic.

"So, if 95 percent of all our purchase decision-making takes place in our subconscious mind, how do we understand what our customers want and why they want it? It's actually quite simple. First, you would have to determine if you know *who* your customer really is. Can you describe *who* your ideal customer is? What really drives him or her? What this person is really passionate about? And why he or she buys?

"Remember that perception *is* reality. Your customer's perception is all that really counts. For example, if you own a restaurant, and it is squeaky clean, and your staff is constantly scrubbing the floors after hours, but the cleaning materials were changed recently to a sterile-smelling formula like one used in a hospital that reminds that customer of the bad food she had at the hospital last month for her appendectomy, her perception of your restaurant's food will cause her to not return again.

"Because the customer is making his decisions at a subconscious level, he is responding with his emotions. How does he view your product or service? Is he pleased, satisfied, unhappy, frustrated, neglected, submissive, interested, feeling important, in control, safe, valued, or happy?

"Understanding your target customers' demographics is important—who they are, including their age, gender, income, and location—but delving into the psychographics seeks to answer the questions of why your customers buy what you sell. What are their attitudes, opinions, and personality traits that motivate them to buy what they do?

"Through the explosion of the Internet universe surrounding our lives, we can unlock unique subcultures, or 'tribes' of individuals who care about a specific thing, an interest, a cause, or an idea, something that will resonate with that particular group on what you are selling, not because you are selling it, but because they have an unconscious need, waiting to find the reason to fulfill it.

"The nexus between their passion and your product or service might be tangential. For example, a group that is passionate about healthy organic fruits also has a strong affinity with bluegrass music. They attend monthly festivals, and they participate in traditional folk music blogs. You can utilize this information to combine these various behavioral elements in context to reach their psychographic target. They may look at advertising on particular music content or music festival sites, or begin to integrate these new topics into their social media strategies.

"Perhaps over time, you can begin to build a more sophisticated profile and targeting strategy by identifying stronger customer buying behaviors with certain bluegrass bands or specific music festivals. So, by including these psychographic elements into your targeting strategies, your marketing efforts can truly lead to greater profits."

"That is so true," agreed Mark. "We have a huge following with fly fishermen with these special fly lures that are made for us exclusively. These guys are also huge barbecue cook-off aficionados. They go to these cook-off festivals, and they all talk about this website on which they show off their latest recipes and who knows what else. I could look into advertising on that website for our fly lures and probably tap into a huge universe of new buyers from all around."

"You could advertise with them, you could write articles on their website, you could sponsor events, or you could even give away samples. Once you know to whom you are marketing, the possibilities are limitless. Actually, Mark, the customer universe doesn't have to be huge. It just has to be spot-on targeted to exactly whom you are trying to attract," Heidi added. "Those in that tribe are whom you want to be targeting, and they will love you for talking directly to them."

"That's right," Scott continued. "Knowing your customers requires listening skills too often forgotten by the entrepreneurial community. By listening, we seek to understand their needs, either directly or, more likely, indirectly by their divulging nuggets of valuable insight that can be applied into our marketing strategies. Listen face-to-face, listen through your employees, listen through social media channels, and listen through online reviews. This used to be done only by large marketing firms that charged a lot of money for these services. But now, with the onset of social media, you can do this psychographic analysis for a fraction of the price.

"By listening to their needs and understanding what customers really want, you may be innovative in providing a product or service that they didn't even know they wanted. Think of the innovation of Apple, from the iPod, to the iPhone, to the iPad. Clearly these products went beyond what its customers wanted, but simply addressed what they *really* wanted. Every innovation in the history of the world combined an uncanny understanding of human needs and the innovative vision to deliver it. Reach into your customers' needs beyond the present, and discover the possibilities."

Scott and Heidi could see that Mark and Melissa were getting it. That entrepreneurial spark of excitement that they said had not been seen in a while was slowly being rekindled. They were beginning to see that their family corner general store could begin to build into a business with customers who wouldn't need to find them only on the corner of Main and Main anymore. They would tap into a world of customers, speaking directly to those who would find their message appealing. They would develop systems around their business to build a sustainable enterprise.

"You realize that building a business like you're talking about will take time," said Melissa, a hint of concern in her voice. "We don't have something like this in place right now."

"Think of the one example Mark shared about the fly-fishing lure customers," Heidi replied. "Mark didn't do any detailed analysis to realize this; it was simply by listening to *your* customers and making the connection between their love of fly-fishing and barbecues. Just imagine the possibilities if you were to give that analysis a little bit more focus, and what that could mean for you to identify more connections with your customers.

"By working *on* your business instead of *for* your business, you give yourself the greatest gift an entrepreneur can give. You are creating something that is enjoyable to build and is a reflection of your values and interests, and once it is built, that business can sustain itself without you. It's almost like parenting, isn't it?"

Chapter 6

THE TECHNOLOGY TOOL BELT

Time is really the only capital that any human being has, and the only thing he can't afford to lose.

—Thomas Edison

"It's kind of daunting to try and build a business that can compete globally with the big boys, isn't it?" remarked Mark.

"On the contrary, Mark," said Scott. "There's never been a better time to be an entrepreneur than today. Don't you realize that technology today, and the low cost of implementing that technology, gives you a tool belt that the big guys only wish they could compete with? The barrier of entry that existed as little as ten years ago has been diminished almost completely.

"You can create an idea, source a manufacturer for the product based on that idea, sell it (even before it's made), design a brand, build a website, disseminate video, create media buzz, blog about it, handle payment processing, and handle order fulfillment as well as distribution—all with no employees, factories, studio facilities, warehouses, packaging, or trucking resources. Just imagine how nervous the big guys are in figuring out how to compete with *you* now."

Don't Fear Technology

"FDR originally said, 'The only thing to fear is fear itself.' Our modern take on this phrase is, 'The only thing we have to fear with technology is fear itself.' Fortunately, we are living in a rather unique period of history that lies at the intersection of productivity and technology. History has had other transformative periods, such as the Industrial Revolution, where hand production methods transformed into machine tools, and then into steam-powered factories.

"But unlike the environment of the late 1700s, the current tool set has created a tool chest of extremely powerful weapons of mass production. It's amazing to realize our reliance today on modern technology tools that actually began in the not-too-distant past. For example, it was in the 1990s that early email providers—such as Pegasus, AOL, Excite, and Hotmail—started. Google began googling in 1998, and by 1999 Google was answering three million searches daily. According to statisticbrain. com, Google currently answers more than one billion questions every day from people around the globe, in 181 countries and 146 languages. YouTube began in 2005, and Facebook started in 2004. And today the number of text messages sent each day exceeds the population of the entire planet. The pace of technology innovation is truly staggering!"

"Amazing, when we realize that twenty years ago we didn't know what Google or a text message was," Heidi added.

"Absolutely!" Scott replied. "Yet, as we look around us today, we are literally drowning in a world of 'always on,' with the plethora of mobile devices, tablets, laptops, Bluetooth accessories, cloud connectivity, and smart TVs. We're no longer in the Information Age; we've moved into the age of over-information. Each year, we create and distribute more information than we have produced in the past five thousand years. Take a moment, and really let that sink in. But the beauty of where this technology train has taken us is that we can finally harness these tools to work smarter, play harder, think sharper, investigate better, hire better, live healthier, navigate straighter, write clearer, learn faster, and communicate more efficiently."

"So what does all that mean to the CoupleCEO?" Melissa questioned.

"Melissa, as you know, the most important underlying theme to everything we teach is to achieve balance in your business and personal life," Scott continued. "Think of technology as your shared tool belt to stay competitive in a world that changes constantly. As an effective team, you and Mark can utilize these powerful weapons to yield results throughout your professional and personal lives. These new information weapons will allow you to focus on what really matters in getting to your goals, but you have to use them wisely so as not to shoot yourselves in the foot with them."

Synchronize Your Daily Activities

"Here are some recommendations we've found to help synchronize and synergize your daily activities and harness these tools without getting caught up in the technology under the hood. Remember, it's like driving a car—the point is to travel from here to there, but as long as the automobile is functioning, you really don't need to get under the hood. And with the advances in automotive engineering these days, there's less and less to really worry about. We realize that software will constantly be changing and improving, but as of today, here are some of the tools in our belt that we believe every CoupleCEO should have:

"The calendar has been around for a long time, and we all have used it. What is different with a calendar that is synced with your CoupleCEO partner is changes to appointments and the daily schedule can be communicated instantly without having to meet with the other person. You can invite your partner to events, either to have him or her attend, or to simply communicate something that you will be attending alone but want to let him or her know about. You can designate these calendar items with an 'Info Only' designation after the event description.

"Calendar applications, such as Outlook, iCal, or Google, allow you to invite others to scheduled appointments and also provide confirmation of the invitees' acceptance. No more 'I told you that I was going to be meeting with Mr. Smith, and I needed you to close the store' or 'Why didn't you tell me about our meeting with the widget vendor?' Just like when driving the car, you can keep your focus on the road, and on getting things done and having more time left at the end of the day.

"Realize that you can also show your partner's complete calendar on yours, with different color-coding, but personally, we find that too distracting. Usually there isn't a limitation on the number of people with whom you can share a calendar. Remember, both of you are focusing on your own goals and objectives—those that are the best match for your own strengths and opportunities. So realize that your calendar will be a reflection of that profile, and use the sharing function to invite your partner to activities that seem relevant to keeping them in the loop.

"Try scheduling date nights, workout sessions, even personal time to get that pedicure . . . . Have fun with it because it really is all about communication, connecting in a way that keeps you both in sync with each other, but doesn't cause tripping over each other all day as well. We keep track of our son's soccer schedules, the Bucs football schedule (home and away), and social events. You'll find you get more things accomplished in your days and your nights."

"I remember being at a meeting with Adam's teacher," Heidi recalls, "and she told me about an upcoming school event. I told her I was going to invite Scott as I pulled out my calendar on my phone, and she was shocked! She said, 'I thought you all worked together.' I told her we do, but that doesn't mean we can read each other's minds. It was much more efficient to invite him then, than to make a note to tell him later."

"Rarely is there an application that we can suggest for CoupleCEOs that's more helpful at keeping track of everything than Evernote," Heidi continues. "It is available for Mac or PC users. It is free and can be downloaded on your smartphone or tablet to be used remotely. This useful tool is a must-have in your tool belt because it keeps track of all the  information that can easily be lost or misplaced in the hectic daily lives of CoupleCEOs. Think of it as a big digital chest of information into which you can keep putting a lot of information. Actually, it's really like a backup brain. Things you see on the Internet; things you take pictures of that are interesting designs or give you ideas for new products; upcoming travel arrangements; meeting notes, including recordings; ideas that pop into your head that you want to write down; inspirational quotes; photos or illustrations; the picture of a price tag for comparison shopping; shopping lists; wish lists; house-hunting notes; a recipe repository; checklists for anything; a picture of a business card; a picture of a white board (before it's erased); or voice notes on anything you want to remember.

"Here's where the magic happens. The information goes out to the Evernote server, where it's processed and indexed, letting you do such things as search for all of your text in images, search by location, and so on. Once you start using it for everything you want to keep track of, you start seeing the benefits of using it. Forget Post-it Notes; this takes information collection to an entirely new level. The ability to search your backup brain for anything you need to find is an extremely powerful tool.

"One of the features it offers is called Web Clipper. As you're researching on the web and find something to save, by clipping it to Evernote, you save it as an article, a simplified article, a full page, a bookmark, or a screenshot. For example, if you clip the simplified article, you now have the article in your Evernote account, organized in a folder, and it can be edited, added to—just like a word processing document. Also, it can be tagged, a reminder can be set up on it, and it shows up in searches in your Evernote account. Heidi and I are always researching new topics to add to our CoupleCEO workshops and CoupleCEO.com content, and throughout our speaking engagements. The Web Clipper allows us to web-surf, finding useful information, and simply click it into a folder for that topic. It eliminates time-consuming note-taking or printing out paper copies of the information to assemble into the article, lesson, or speech. It's just waiting in our Evernote folder on the topic. Just imagine what we can do with the time saved.

"Additionally, business cards can be saved, which become searchable with Evernote's optical character recognition; recipes and restaurant recommendations, receipts and serial numbers of big purchases can be saved; and you can archive whiteboard notes from your meetings or brainstorming sessions. As a simple example, say you archived a recipe, and you want to pull it up, but all you remember is that it had kale in it. Query 'kale' on the app on your phone while at the grocery store, and it will find it for you. This is much more efficient than going through all of your cookbooks or bookmarked recipes on your computer. You can attach spreadsheets or text documents, anything you want to save in your big digital chest of information, your backup brain.

"I am sure when you all go to a trade show, you collect tons of brochures and business cards, and you shove them all in the bags they provide for you. You get back to the store, and you know there was a product you were interested in; you have to dump out the bag and cull through all of that information to find it. In Evernote, you create a folder; take pictures of the business cards, brochures, or actual products; and they are automatically archived for you with the proper indexing.

"Another feature is the ability to share notebooks. This is perfect for staying in sync with your partner on a project, a new client prospect, a conference you both are attending, a new parcel of land you are looking to develop, a trip you are planning, your grocery list . . . . Instead of a 'honey-do list,' make it a 'couple-do list' (heck, even your life bucket list)—put anything and everything you want to store into that big digital chest of information.

"One cool feature is that you set up an email address within Evernote, where you can email anything to, and it shows up in your default notebook. It's helpful to make this default notebook @Inbox because it shows up at the top of the alphabetical listing, and you can sort out where you want to file it from there, if you want.

"This tool is ideal because it resides on your laptop, your tablet, your smartphone, and even your desktop computer—and it all synchronizes into the same account, wherever you are. It's like having a dozen assistants keeping notes for you, photographing things you want to document, recording things you want to hear later, filing it all into a great big filing room and retrieving it when you need something. The more you use Evernote, the more you won't know what you did without it.

"For years, we had file servers at our office, storing all of our design files, contracts, photography, documents, spreadsheets, presentations, everything—on this oversized computer sitting in the corner by the copier. And we had tape backups every night, a different one every night, and one tape had to be stored off site each week, and the tapes wore out, and the file server constantly needed updates and upgrades, or went down because the UPS (uninterrupted power supply) battery had to be replaced, and on, and on, and on . . . .

"And on the seventh day, God created Dropbox! Well, not exactly, but it was heaven-sent, for sure. Now, all of our files are stored in the cloud. Cloud storage is simply an off-site storage

 system maintained by a third party. Thanks to the cloud, all of your data can be stored off-site. In addition to not having to maintain servers in your office or store, you can access your data from wherever you are. The Internet provides the connection between you and your database.

"We have files wherever we need them, from our desktop, laptop, tablet, or smartphones. See a theme going on here? Dropbox does the heavy lifting of handling our files, sorted by folders, of course. We can share a link to a file with other people. We can control the setting of the shared folder either to view files only or to be allowed to modify them.

"This tool allows us to collaborate on projects with others. For example, home-building clients have a folder to which they can upload pictures of kitchen cabinets they like, or plumbing fixtures for the bathroom. We can place all of the project paperwork there, from closing statements, to contract documents, to change orders on the job.

"I am assuming that your manufacturer's reps don't come and visit you at the store the way they did twenty or thirty years ago, correct?" asked Heidi.

"Several of the companies we work with have scaled back to the point that they only go to the trade shows," Mark answered.

"So just imagine being able to share a file with them that shows them some remodeling you are planning to do and how you are reorganizing the section that promotes their product. They could provide you with feedback and might even have some ad hoc dollars to help you with the expense. All of this happens without their ever needing to set foot in the door," Heidi said. "I miss the face-to-face connection that's often being lost, but this is a way to pull them into your business by using these tools."

Scott continued, "Rather than email an attachment document to a client, we can simply add a Dropbox link to the email that allows them to download the file. For large files, this is much easier than waiting for the mail to go through the email outbox queue. We could have a video file that wouldn't be able to be emailed. Providing a Dropbox link is a solution that is easy and efficient.

"Backups on our end have been eliminated, as have server maintenance costs and potential downtime. By having access to all of our files wherever we are, they are waiting for us just an Internet connection away, thanks to the cloud."

"So the common theme here, Scott, so far, as I understand it, is that your information becomes shared and synchronized as a couple, so you can effectively collaborate on work and personal life," summarized Melissa.

"I don't think I could say it better myself!" beamed Scott. "I think we have some room in our tool belt for some more technology. Let's fill it up.

"We have found it helpful to have several shared email accounts, along with our own email addresses, to facilitate communication to clients or outside organizations that need to communicate with both of us regarding some matters, whether business or personal. Setting up these as Gmail accounts is an easy way to facilitate this, although you could always handle this through your own domain account as well. In fact, having email accounts, such as info@domain.com or warranty@domain. com (filling in your domain for the domain.com, of course), is a great way of directing specific inquiries or communications to specific departments in your business.

"As we share certain email accounts, we can both be receiving or sending communication as the combined voice of both of us— something that is very effective as a CoupleCEO. It is much more effective than simply copying the other on correspondence. It says to the recipient, 'We are talking with a single voice here, and you can reply and be sure that we both are listening to what you're saying to us.'

"Another great use of a shared email is the opt-in account, which allows you to provide email information for opt-ins or for additional information you're receiving. You may be hesitant to share email information at times in return for receiving content you may be interested in, or you may simply want to test out something before giving your actual information. The shared opt-in account allows you to safely dip your toe in the waters of the World Wide Web to explore and to learn.

"By separating these accounts, you are organizing your day. The opt-in emails, for example, are really only for research, so you don't flood your inbox with them. Turn those off during the day, and only read those when the time is right. People spend as much time not being productive reading opt-in emails as they do looking at friends' daily escapades on Facebook. Remember, the goal is to reduce the time so that you can start enjoying your time savings in other ways.

"Along with your shared Gmail account, you now have the ability to share the Chrome browser within the Google suite of products. We have more than one browser on our computers, but we find Chrome to be the best option for shared information. The beauty of this marriage is that bookmarking is shared within the Chrome browser, so each person could be researching new product line ideas, for example, and bookmarking the sites under a folder called New Products. When each person comes up with something that looks interesting, he or she can save it to the same folder.

"Now, remember that within your technology tool belt, there will always be some overlap of tools that can handle similar things. With the example previously discussed about sharing bookmarked sites, the CoupleCEO also has Evernote's amazing functionality of taking interesting websites, and placing the content onto a Note. Remember, the difference here is that with Evernote, you could be saving just the content only, or you could be saving a link bookmark to the website. Your choices, your bullets; choose your weapon.

"Of course, the most robust and powerful weapon in this tool belt has to be the smartphone. Your smartphone allows you to  virtually take your work anywhere both of you care to be—on a boat, by the pool, on the beach, or anywhere you would care to go (notice our water theme?)."

"Scott," said Heidi, "think of how many times we are using Skype on our phones with our team in India or the Philippines while we're having lunch, or we're checking pricing for something on Amazon while we're in another store shopping, or even on FaceTime with a colleague while out of the office. It's amazing to realize our dependence on phones for the versatility they allow us in conducting business wherever we are."

"Exactly, Heidi," Scott said. "It's amazing to realize that all of the tools we have spoken about so far can reside on your smartphone sitting in your pocket or your purse. It is not limited to a one-to-one communication device as it was when it weighed five pounds and had to be carried on your shoulder with a strap. By learning to become proficient with your smartphone, both of you can extend your work boundaries to shave significant hours from your workday and spend that time investing in your relationship and yourself.

"I would much rather reply to that email briefly on my phone in the late afternoon while playing cards with Heidi at home, or while having a nice sunset sail, instead of being strapped to handle that work behind my desk. By extending your mind-set into what and when is work time, and allowing yourself to handle certain tasks that lend themselves to out-of-office productivity, consider the incremental gains you can make in your daily work life.

"Here are some examples of smartphone solutions that you might not have considered:

- You can make three-way calls to clarify business points in a contract among all parties while you are traveling to a sales call.
- You can know the exact time of arrival at your designated meeting based on traffic conditions.
- By using the proper commands, you can ask your automated assistant (for example, Siri) to:
  o 'SEND' your wife a message you'll be right there.
  o 'GIVE' you directions to the prospect's office.
  o 'POST' something to Facebook.
  o 'REMIND' you to call your mom.
  o 'EMAIL' your brother.
  o 'NOTE' that you spent $12 on lunch.
  o 'ADD' an Evernote reminder.
- Your phone can be a replacement for your wallet.
  o Eliminate the need to carry cash or credit cards by downloading a digital wallet app that will allow you to pay by waving, sliding, or tapping.
- Identify things, such as products, famous landmarks, storefronts, artwork, and other popular images, including celebrities, using an app built into Google called Goggles. Try using this the next time you're stumped to place a name with that actor in the TV episode you're watching.

Just pause the screen, take a shot of the person using Google Goggles, and wham! Talk about total recall.

- Watch live TV on the go. Need we say more?

- Use the phone as a universal remote control. Get rid of all the remote clutter as well as the 'Who's got the remote?' arguments at the same time.

- Accept credit card purchases using such applications as Square that provide a hassle-free and inexpensive way for any business to accept credit card payments from customers. A small dongle attaches onto your phone to accept credit card swipes.

- Wearables, which can be worn as necklaces, as bracelets, on a belt loop—you name it, describe ancillary attachments that work with the smartphone. They can be used to track your steps taken, your distance traveled, calories burned, and so on."

Scott watched Mark and Melissa as they were absorbing all of this. "I never thought about using my phone for so many different things," Melissa admitted. "This certainly shines a new light on it."

Mark added, "We had been considering the Square application to handle overflow at the cash register. Scott makes it sound so simple; I think maybe we should."

"All of these tools are great to add to your tool belt," said Scott. "But you still need some basic organization and prioritizing in order to efficiently accomplish everything you set out to accomplish. Time management is definitely worth mastering. The results are extremely fulfilling."

Scott and Heidi explained to Mark and Melissa their Couple Priority Planning and Personal Productivity methodology. "There are two that we recommend. They work together, one for the couple, and one for each person. The methodology for Couple Priority Planning involves ordering your tasks into A's, B's, and C's. We use an integrated system with our iPhones and iPads. The app is called 'Benjamin—a Franklin style task manager.' Both of us load this smartphone app synchronized to the same account. Therefore, we are both managing our tasks together. Tasks and Projects can really include anything. For us, they include homebuilding projects, CoupleCEO projects, and even family and personal projects."

By adding tasks to each project, they showed Mark and Melissa how they created a priority hierarchy of A, B, and C tasks inside their related projects. The application could drag a task up or down in priority, allowing it to be an A1, A2, or A3. The A tasks *must* be done by the end of the day. The B tasks *should* be done by the end of the day. And the C tasks *could* get done by the end of the day. Scott showed how by adding a task on his phone, and it would appear on Heidi's phone. Mark and Melissa were impressed with this wonderful time management methodology as an excellent system to coordinate tasks between the CoupleCEO.

"Additionally, we utilize a Personal Productivity methodology individually, based on the best-selling book *Getting Things Done,* by David Allen," Heidi says. "In getting tasks accomplished for a project, GTD˚ focuses in on defining what is our Next Action to be accomplished. It organizes our Next Actions into a series of folders or notebooks based on the context—the people, places, and tools needed to get the work done. Our collection of Next

Action notebooks is reviewed weekly to stay abreast of all the stuff that needs to be done.

"Evernote acts as an excellent tool to manage these notebooks. The ease of capturing information through this program, and then being able to manage your Next Actions, complete with time and date deadlines, if necessary, allows you to stay focused on the task at hand quickly and efficiently. You even can email items directly into specific notebooks, or use the Web Clipper to sweep information into your next actions.

"Scott and I find that combining these two approaches, using the shared application to keep track of our collective work, as well as managing individual Next Action notebooks for each of our responsibilities, we are able to utilize time management practices that result in more work to get more done in less time. Additionally, as new ideas and opportunities present themselves, we have a way to immediately capture them to later sort and shine a light on what we need to focus upon."

"Speaking of shining a light, of course, we can't forget the flashlight app for the phone! I've used that one more times than I can count!" exclaimed Scott. "But just remember, technology will continue to speed ahead with so many new toys and tools for us to share. It's not so important to stay on the very cutting edge of this phenomena, but it is important to remain open-minded and flexible in our business and personal lives to embrace the ways technology will allow us to spend more time on the important aspects of our existence. As it frees us up from tasks that can be automated or simplified, we will need to explore how we can use our creativity tools and innovation to continue to grow exponentially throughout our lives."

"Everyone in our CoupleCEO community stays connected to the latest technology tools for their tool belt through www.CoupleCEO.com," reminded Heidi. "Our members enjoy the experience of an interactive website complete with education, conversation, and participation."

Chapter 7

Healthy Deposits

It is health that is real and not pieces of gold and silver.
—Mahatma Gandhi

Mark and Melissa watched Scott and Heidi as they raised the sails. *Grand Cru* leaped at the opportunity as the wind led them on a southbound tack into Tampa Bay. As Heidi coiled the lines neatly inside the cockpit, Melissa asked curiously, "So how do you find the time to keep so fit, eat right, and have all this energy? I'm tired just watching you move all around the boat."

Unlock Your Energy

"Actually, eating right and staying fit is exactly why we have the energy we have," replied Heidi, smiling. "You need to think of it as an investment you're making, a small incremental daily investment that will continue to yield an ongoing return over time. Think of it as the best investment you can make in your entire life, one that has a residual return and a payout that will reward you over time, an investment that can be leveraged into a multitude of productive ways, amassing wealth in ways that result in doing great things."

"Absolutely," Scott agreed. "The best investment in terms of the returns it brings. This investment isn't in gold, or stocks, or even bonds. And no, it's not in real estate. It's an investment with a far greater yield than any of the others combined. It's an investment in your health, both of yours, of course. It's the food that you eat, the exercise that you do, and even the sex that you have. Think of all of these as contributions into your own personal 401(k) health bank account."

"Now, we aren't trying to turn all of you into fitness fanatics or health food aficionados," clarified Heidi, "but we do want to stress the vital importance of these lessons to maximize the returns in both your businesses and your relationships."

"That's right," Scott said. "We weren't always in balance when it came to proper nutrition and exercise practice, but as we learned the foundations of all of these components, the building blocks and why things worked the way they did, we learned why it was helping to produce our energy and our creativity, as well as eliminating the stress we were experiencing. By getting that constant feedback, it made us continue to learn about what worked and kept us following the patterns we were creating. I guess when you're on the path, and it feels pretty good, you really don't want to get off of it, do you?"

Diet Is a Noun, not a Verb

"So what's the secret on eating?" asked Melissa. "I just seem to swing from one diet to the next, and it doesn't seem to stick. . . . I lose weight, but then I put it back on, like a yo-yo. I'm just tired of dieting—it's affecting my focus on running our store, and I just seem to be tired all the time."

"First of all, let's talk about the meaning of the word 'diet,'" Heidi began. "According to dictionary.com, the definition is: (v.) 'To eat and drink according to a regulated system, especially so as to lose weight.' The problem with this is that it is temporary. Once you complete the goal of losing weight, the diet ceases— and Melissa, you just affirmed what we all know happens next: the weight comes back on. We prefer to see the word 'diet' as a noun. Again, here is the definition from dictionary.com: (n.) 'The usual food and drink of a person or animal.' You should no longer consider a diet to be a temporary action, but your daily eating."

"Here's an idea," Scott said. "Let's just talk about the joy of eating, and cooking, and trying out new recipes, and exploring new cuisines. Let's just bring the fun back into what we put in our mouths."

Heidi smiled as she looked at the others, and continued, "And as we start to understand what different foods do to us, and how they work together and combine in the most amazing ways, we find our balance—our body equilibrium.

"Remember back to your childhood and the three basic food groups: proteins, carbohydrates, and fats. There were other

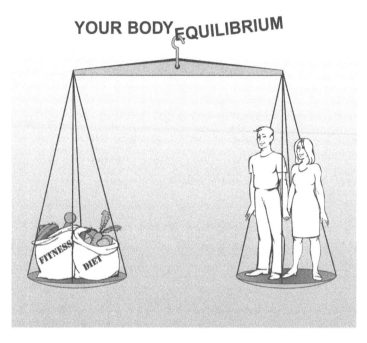

components that probably were discussed as well, but let's just keep it simple with these three. Your body needs a combination of all three of these groups with every meal to really feel right—a perfect combination doesn't leave you hungry, wanting more, or lethargic from eating too much, but just like with Goldilocks, it is just right.

"See, there's a biological reason for this, but without getting too technical and over the top, your food is like a drug. By eating the right combinations of your three food groups, you are essentially taking the proper drug dose to maintain the right hormone balance and keep your blood sugar stable."

"So it's simply about the right combination of food groups that makes this work?" asked Melissa cautiously.

"That's right," answered Scott. "You see, it's really all about insulin. The pancreas releases insulin after you eat carbohydrates. That's the insulin response. It assures that your cells receive the necessary blood sugar—but it also converts almost half of your carbohydrates directly into fat and causes hunger.

"There are really two types of carbohydrates—the good ones, which are vegetables and fruits, and the bad ones, which are the breads, pastas, rice, potatoes, and so on. Basically, everything that is refined has these refined sugars that really get that insulin spiking.

"So you're just combining these good carbs with some protein and adding some fat, such as olive oil, avocado, or peanut butter. You keep your body in balance and your insulin response in moderation. You don't get tired, or hungry, or stuffed. And you try to eat some *between meals* as well."

"You mean snacking all day?" asked Mark.

"No, not all day," replied Heidi. "Just try to add two snacks into your normal day, as well as your breakfast, lunch, and dinner, so that you keep the insulin levels steady throughout the day. Mid-morning and mid-afternoon snacks normally do the trick. It's the swings that really lead all of us to have cravings and eat what we regret afterward. Whether it's protein bars, or cottage cheese with an apple and peanut butter, it's really just about maintaining that balance, from meals to snacks, with your proteins, carbohydrates, and fats. It's a great combination, and you'll feel great in eating this way."

"Remember that you need to have that same balance of proteins, carbohydrates, and fats in all of your meals, not just your snacks," Scott said. "An easy way to implement this type of eating at meals is to think of your plate in thirds. **One-third of the plate will consist of** a low-fat protein that is no bigger than the palm of your hand. This can be chicken, lean meat, turkey, pork, or fish. Then fill the **other two-thirds of the plate** with colorful carbohydrates (vegetables and fruits). Finally, add a dash (that's a small amount) of fat that is low in omega-6 and saturated fats, such as olive oil. Simple in concept, but often difficult because you will have to avoid many of the 'starchy carbs' that people love to eat (bread, pizza, pasta, potatoes, and rice)."

THE HEALTHY PLATE

Fruits & Vegetables

Low Fat Protein

Monounsaturated Fats

"Yep, that's the food that I crave the most—pizza and potato chips," Mark agreed.

"That's why it's so important to remember that you have to maintain that appropriate balance of proteins, carbohydrates, and fats at every meal," described Heidi. "By keeping that balance, you keep the insulin response in check—your body isn't dealing with a lot of bad carbohydrates and turning those carbs into your body's fat reserve. You are actually regulating the hormonal balance that Scott spoke of. The first three weeks without starchy carbs, you probably will be thinking about starches a lot. But after three weeks, as your body has gradually tapered off the urges, you will have the habit of not craving those bad carbs. In fact, just wait till the first time you sit in a restaurant and the breadbasket is served. You'll be amazed to find that you will automatically say no and have no regrets, or cravings. It won't be a painful no; it will be natural."

"Oh, and remember . . . water, water, water," she continued. "Get rid of those diet sodas and fruit drinks. Diet soda and artificial sweeteners can disrupt the body's natural ability to regulate calorie intake based on the sweetness of foods. So you're actually more likely to overeat because your body is being tricked into thinking it's eating sugar, and you actually crave more.

"Besides, remember that you lose fluids throughout the day, and drinking water helps maintain that balance of your body fluids. It energizes our muscles, helps our skin look good through proper hydration, and makes the kidneys work properly in cleansing and ridding the body of toxins."

"And, Heidi, let's not forget that adequate hydration keeps everything flowing along the gastrointestinal tract, leading to a normal bowel function. A good way to start my day, isn't it?" Scott said. "And as we are aging, helping this to function properly is very important."

"Right, Scott," Heidi said. "Your day hasn't begun before you've *finished* your morning routine." Mark laughed.

"It's very important to support each other in maintaining good, healthy eating," Scott encouraged. "It's really a team sport. Many couples consider this to be nagging. But it is not nagging; your spouse is your cheerleader or your coach to help you optimize your body. Instead of looking at it negatively, consider it in the perspective that you are both making deposits into your personal 401(k) health bank account. If either one of you misses a deposit, it really affects both of you as a team—from a business perspective as well as a personal relationship perspective. Helping each of you to become the best you can be provides you with the energy, the creativity, and the passion you bring to both of your lives."

"I guess I never really looked at it that way," admitted Melissa. "I was approaching my dieting attempts as simply fitting into a certain dress, or just looking better to myself in the mirror. I wasn't seeing diet as something to pay into consistently for a long-term perspective. But I agree that this is a refreshing way to approach it."

Mark said, "But before turning fifty-ish, I didn't think much about my diet. I had been very fortunate that I remained healthy without much focus on what I ate. But over the past five years, I've started to notice that I'm more sluggish than I used to be. And obviously more things hurt when I'm lifting things in the store and generally exerting myself—hurt more than ever before."

"Well, you're lucky, you lasted a few more years than we did," Heidi recounted. "For us, it was in our mid-40s when the transition began to happen. Suddenly, playing soccer with our boys caused us to get out of breath more quickly. And the clothes that I had been wearing for the past 10 years were getting tight. There are hundreds of studies that verify that your metabolism changes every decade; some studies say it's every 7 years. One study explained, "If at 25 you weighed 130 pounds and ran 3 miles 5 times a week, at age 45 you'd need to run about 4.5 miles 5 times a week to maintain that weight and not diet." So what you are experiencing is normal, and you don't need to blame yourself; you simply need to adjust your routine and probably think a little bit more about what foods you put into your system."

"We have always eaten fairly healthy," said Scott. "We've never been fanatical, but we've been just practical—no Cheetos or Oreo cookies, always vegetables with lunch and dinner, avoid fast food, and so on. So based on our decent eating along with semi-regular exercise, our weight and physical shape had remained somewhat constant. But once we reached the 'other side of the hill,' what was once constant was not so anymore.

"So we knew that our semi-regular exercise needed to become a daily routine. Once we committed to that, our energy level improved significantly. As we have interviewed CoupleCEOs about their exercise routines, we have gotten a mixed response as to whether couples should work out or exercise together. Therefore, you need to decide what is best for your lifestyle."

"That's right," said Heidi. "For example, Scott and I really enjoy working out together, and we enjoy different types of exercise, so each of us is a good motivator for the other. Scott enjoys jogging, and I abhor it. I love to lift weights, and do pushups, sit-ups, and so on. We exercise outside on a sidewalk that is seven miles long. When Scott exercises alone, he jogs the whole path. When I exercise alone, I power walk and stop along the way to do pushups, step-ups, and so on. When we exercise together, we push each other to do those exercises that are not part of our normal routine.

"I would do the same routine every day for a year and not get bored with it," Heidi continued. "But ask any physical trainer, and he will tell you that you need to vary your routine to keep the muscles stronger; otherwise, the other muscles in your body will degenerate. Scott, on the other hand, gets bored with routines quickly, so he is always researching new and varied routines. These are some of the reasons that for us, working out together is a benefit. But remember that whether you exercise together or exercise apart, it needs to become a weekly or daily occurrence. It needs to be a habit."

Melissa looked at Mark and sighed. "Listen, I know that what you are saying makes sense, but we haven't had exercise in our lives since we were in our twenties. I am concerned that our bodies can't handle vigorous exercise."

"We're not suggesting vigorous exercise," Heidi replied. "You just need to get up and move around more than what you are currently doing, and make it a routine. Of course, you should always check with your physician in case there are any exercises that he or she recommends you avoid, especially if you have had any kind of a preexisting condition.

"In fact, research now points to the role that exercise plays in shedding excess fat. Working out is the key—whether it's running, jumping, lifting, or playing a sport. Just find a way to elevate your heart rate and force your muscles to work hard. In other words, find ways to build up muscle mass because once you have that muscle mass, you can use it to attack the fat that covers it up. Does that make sense?"

Mark nodded, "Yeah, I can understand that. But I've really never been into weight lifting and stuff like that at the gym," he admitted.

"But we're not just talking weight lifting, Mark," answered Scott. "There are plenty of core muscle body exercises that Heidi and I do that build muscle mass and, in the process, help to burn the excess fat in the body. In addition, the many benefits of exercise go way beyond just the effects on weight. It can be great for stress reduction, improved insulin sensitivity, and other hormonal responses to food (remember, we talked about the insulin response on fat production). Plus, exercise gives you an overall sense of competence and accomplishment, with those endorphins rushing through your system, and it gives you the motivation to improve other behaviors. Also important to remember as we age is that elderly people who are physically fit have a much better survival rate after those later-in-life challenges than do those who are dormant."

"As a CoupleCEO, you need to work on many aspects of your life to connect the pieces, and good health is a very important piece," Heidi added. "But since exercise hasn't been part of your routine in more than twenty years, let us provide some tips to make the transition easier and simple to implement.

"Here are some tips to help you begin to get active:

- Don't use the excuse 'I don't have time.'
  o Twenty minutes is a great period of time.
  o Even ten-minute workouts will do.
- Start slow.
  o If you haven't had an exercise regimen, start slow.

- o   Walk before you jog.
- o   Start with five-pound weights, and build up from there.
- o   Start with two ten-minute workouts per day.
- o   If you're joining a class, try one per week.
- Commit to a routine, and stick with it.
  - o   Make an exercise date at least four days per week.
  - o   Stick with it at least three weeks. By then, it will be a habit.
- Give yourself short-term goals.
  - o   Don't make the goals about weight loss.
  - o   Make the goals about energy level.
- Do what you enjoy.
  - o   You have so many options—yoga, walking, swimming, and more.
  - o   If you enjoy it, it will be a pleasure to make it a habit."

"We always exercise when on vacation, even more than at home," Scott said. "We love the energy it gives us to enjoy our vacation. Remember that as you get older, joints and muscles become sore more readily than in your youth. But this is not a reason to slow down your exercise. Just the opposite: this is exactly why you must exercise daily. It is important to keep the muscles strong now more than ever. The most rewarding part of beginning a fitness routine is noticing the difference it makes in the rest of your life. Even if you begin exercising with a few simple stretches while seated or a short walk around the block, you'll notice an improvement in how you feel as you go about your day.

"So by eating better, with the appropriate balance of healthy carbohydrates, fats, and lean proteins, you will see your cravings go away, and those carb crashes will disappear. Combine that with your new exercise habit, and you will become more energized at work and at home. You will discover a new energy level that will become contagious, and I bet you will find yourself smiling more too.

"So have these suggestions inspired you to start depositing in your 401(k) health account?" Scott asked with a grin. "We'll help you get started today with our healthy meal while we're at our lunchtime anchorage."

Chapter 8

THE ART OF INTIMACY

They slipped briskly into an intimacy from which they never recovered.
—**F. Scott Fitzgerald**, *This Side of Paradise*

The sailboat glided gently into the cove as Scott prepared the anchor at the bow and Heidi took the helm, a gentle hum of the engine heard in the cockpit. "Go ahead and put her in neutral," Scott called out. Heidi adjusted the throttle as she held the wheel with one hand. Scott slowly lowered the anchor into the clear, sparkling waters beneath his reflection. He walked back into the cockpit and announced the next item on the day's discussions with their client couple.

What Is Intimacy?

"We have covered a lot of topics so far today," said Scott. "We appreciate your focus, candor, and, of course, your questions. Now comes the topic that occasionally makes people clam up—stay with us, and let's keep up the dialogue. It is time to talk about intimacy."

Mark reached out to take Melissa's hand, caressing it as he looked at her. Melissa's focus stayed on the cockpit table. She shifted in her seat and adjusted the pillow on her back as Mark exchanged looks with Scott. From the lines in the corner of Mark's deep green eyes, he seemed to be concealing a small grin.

"I've been looking forward to this part of the session," Mark smiled.

Melissa chimed in, "Did you tell us earlier that you had some wine onboard? I think I might like a glass about now."

As everyone admired the tranquil setting of the anchorage cove, it grew quiet without the engine, the sails, and the sailing motion around them. Scott poured the Pouilly-Fuissé, a cold white burgundy, one of their favorites for midday anchorages. It had a refreshing taste, a complexity of minerals, vanilla, and citrus, with a bit of unique terroir that only burgundies can claim. The lunch spread that Heidi laid out for everyone looked delicious. Everyone agreed that it was the perfect beginning to the insightful conversation ahead. All eyes shifted onto Heidi as the anticipation built for the next discussion.

"As we told you earlier, we are not couples therapists, and not sex therapists; we leave that to Dr. Ruth," Heidi said. "So we are not here today to analyze you or your relationship. No personal questions will be asked of you, but we need you to chime in and share as you see best. You see, the reason we were inspired to begin working with CoupleCEOs was because friends and associates over the years were amazed that we were so happy going from the bedroom to the boardroom and back. The common thread that we continue to find among other successful CoupleCEOs is the acknowledgment that intimacy is a vital and intentional component to their lives.""I have a question for both of you," Heidi said. "Have you ever thought about what intimacy is for both of you?"

Melissa looked at Mark somewhat puzzled, and both returned their attention to Heidi, like students eager to learn the next topic.

"Think of intimacy as that action, touch, expression, look, scent, or shared thought that ignites a connectedness between the both of you and reaffirms your position as a couple," Heidi continued. "It can be anything, really, but it has to be able to spark a feeling of unity between both of you in order to truly create intimacy."

"Exactly," agreed Scott. "It can be when you're both alone, or when you're in a stadium full of people. It could even be looking at each other across a crowded room. But when Heidi talks about a spark, that's exactly what it is. Think of the spark that you both had when you were first dating, that feeling of connectedness when you found ways that you were alike, things you both were interested in together, foods you both enjoyed eating, or a trail you both always enjoyed hiking together."

Ignite the Spark Daily

"When we think about keeping intimacy in a relationship, or finding ways to bring it back into a relationship, normally, it's all really about finding the things that bring that spark into the things you already do. You're awake maybe sixteen hours a day, right? What common intersections can you both create throughout your day by coming together and doing something that can spark that intimate flame that fuels the relationship fire?

"Here are some ideas:

- Hold hands walking into the office.
- Play footsies under the table in the boardroom.
- Make your favorite recipe together for dinner, and lick each other's fingers when tasting.
- Rub your partner's neck while riding an elevator.
- Smell her perfume behind her earlobe, and end with a kiss.
- Admire her in the mirror as she's getting ready to go out.
- Take a picnic lunch to your favorite park, and feed each other.
- Fold the sheets together.

"These simple gestures can create a rush of oxytocin through your body. Oxytocin is a brain chemical that produces feelings of trust and attachment. During orgasm, this flows through your body in an incredibly powerful way, but also men get a blast of it when they kiss, and women feel a rush when they hold their partner's hand. There are countless other ways that the same chemical can flow in the course of our daily lives. We just have to search for the opportunities."

"Intimacy also can be experienced through an exchange of thoughts, sharing ideas, and enjoying the similarities and differences of your opinions," reminded Heidi. "Each has to be open and receptive to understanding the other's thoughts and emotions, and to be able to open up and share himself or herself. Exposing yourself like that can be a very intimate moment for a couple."

"Activities can be intimate as well," added Scott. "Think of the card games Heidi and I spoke of earlier. We get into playing gin, but more importantly, we are in an activity together, focused together on the rhythm of the game, leaving distractions, such as emails and cell phones, aside, and in the process, we are focusing on each other. Working on puzzles is a similar process. Two sets of eyes are looking at a table full of puzzle pieces, and with each time connecting one of them, it's a small victory for both of you. I have to admit that Heidi is much better at the puzzles than I am, but it's still fun to engage in the activity together."

"This really makes a lot of sense to me," Melissa chimed in. "Sometimes I think we both forget that being intimate together and connected is so much more than just our sex life."

"The reason creating intimate moments for a CoupleCEO is so important is because it often tends to be neglected," Heidi said. "Your lives are intertwined throughout the day and night. Non-CoupleCEOs are more likely to plan a date night as part of their weekly commitment than entrepreneurial couples that work together. You need to be conscious to not allow intimate moments to be forgotten. Just as you make time to get together and discuss your business, you need to make time for your intimacy. Make times where you can be alone together in a situation where you can focus on each other and on your relationship.

"Just remember," Heidi reminded, "there's intimacy that both of you can plan together, but there's also the random, unexpected acts of intimacy that are important too. For example, don't try and just show up with intimacy expressions on the 'Hallmark holidays.' What I mean is, it cannot be occasional, and it should never feel contrived. You need to remember that intimacy can and should be part of each and every day. And random and unexpected acts of intimacy are perfectly fine and highly encouraged."

Scott interjected: "I made the mistake of sending Heidi flowers on Valentine's Day once. I'll never do that again! It certainly wasn't at all random."

"Intimacy needs to be sincere, and no, I'm typically not a cliché person, but if I received flowers or a card *only* on the Hallmark holidays, I would go ballistic," said Heidi. "I would make the very insensitive assumption that you only thought to do this because you received an email from ProFlowers.com that reminded you, or from a commercial you saw. Valentine's Day—don't even think about sending me flowers then. It's just too predictable, and the complete opposite of being random. But sure, give a card for a holiday. But what if it's the first thing he sees in the morning by the mirror when he gets out of bed? Sneak a bit of unpredictability into a predictable Valentine's card."

"I remember the time you put a Valentine's card in my briefcase when I was going on a business trip," remembered Scott, smiling. "It was the first thing I saw on the plane once we were in the air and I was pulling out work. Now, that was an intimate moment, and I was thirty thousand feet in the air!"

"So the lesson is intimacy should be random, heartfelt, and not only in February, May, and your birthday month," reminded Heidi. "Some of the most special cards I've received from Scott are ones in which he's written a poem or a short letter to me expressing his feelings.

"You can't make the mistake of only sharing sweet thoughts on holiday cards or just holding hands on date night. Here are some suggestions:

- **Tell your partner every day you love him or her.** Hopefully this is already happening, but if not start immediately. Don't force it or schedule it. Don't only say it when you wake up in the morning or when you hang up the phone. Be random—pop your head into your partner's office, and simply say, 'I love you.'

- **Send endearing messages at random.** In the middle of the day, send a text message or email that only says, 'I love you!' Scott was flying home once and sent me a text message that read, 'I'm looking forward to seeing you.' Do you have any idea how amazing that made me feel? We had been married more than fifteen years, but I got the same pang I felt when he said sweet things like that when we were dating. I immediately felt loved and appreciated. I remember it vividly. I was at lunch with a girlfriend, and that message came through. She saw the huge grin on my face and asked me what was up. My reply was simply, 'My husband is so incredible.'

- **Hold hands.** Remember when you were young and dating for the first time, and how incredibly special it felt when your date grabbed your hand? That amazing feeling still exists today. Don't we all get a big smile and a pang in our hearts when we see an elderly couple *still* holding hands? It's because we admire that after several decades together, they still express their love for each other. There is something electrifying about having two hands interlock—it says, 'We are connected.'

- **Commit to daily PDAs** (public displays of affection). You love each other, right? Well, why hide it from the world? You don't have to grab your spouse and lay a French kiss on her in the middle of a meeting. The expressions don't even have to be public to everyone. For example, one of the CoupleCEOs that we interviewed talked about how fun it was to simply brush up against each other in a sensual way in the middle of the workday. Remember that intimacy does not have to be limited to outside of business hours.

- **Take ten minutes to do something you know your partner appreciates.** Does your spouse really like to sit and enjoy a cup of coffee together with you in the morning, but you typically want to rush off and get the day started? If so, on occasion, take that ten minutes, and sit with your partner in the morning just because you know he or she likes it. I am that rushing wild coyote in the morning. When I slow down for a moment and sit with Scott, I know it gives him a better start to his day, and it is a quiet way of saying, 'I care about you.' Another simple idea is when you are sitting on the couch, relaxing, watching your favorite show, grab your spouse's foot, and give a foot massage.

- **Give a compliment every day.** You love your partner. You respect your partner. There are things specifically about him or her that you love and respect—tell your partner. I have to admit that this is my weakness; I don't receive compliments well, so therefore, I don't give them often either. I am good with employees, but not as much with my family. If your spouse solved a technological problem that helped you to communicate with your customers more efficiently, tell him how good it was. If your spouse looks particularly good in bright blue, but typically wears black, compliment her on the blue shirt—I bet you will see her wearing that color more often.

- **Cuddle.** When you watch TV together, cuddle. When you are at a friend's house, sitting on the couch, sit close, and hold hands. Just think: you might inspire others. In bed at the end of the day, hold each other; place a head on a shoulder. These are all ways to cuddle and to remind each other, 'I care about you.'

"Remember the golden rule about no business talk at the dinner table?" asked Heidi. "Equally, if not more, important is to extend that rule during intimate moments too. If you have made the quiet time to focus on each other and your relationship, don't mess that up by bringing up business."

"But you want to say it out loud before you forget it," Melissa said.

"I completely understand that feeling," Heidi replied, "but whether it is business, or picking up your prescription at the pharmacy, this is not the time. This is the time that you and your spouse should be focused on the intimacy of the moment. Intimacy should not be cluttered with mundane tasks of the day."

She gave off a glimmer that seemed to say, "I get it."

"When you are a CoupleCEO running a business together, it's easy to let the business run you," Scott explained. "We've discussed this a lot throughout our time together today. You need to run the business, and if the business is entering your bedroom, then you have fallen into the trap of letting the business run you at one of the worst possible times, and it's time to fix it!"

Both Scott and Heidi were sensing that this conversation was slowly sinking in to both Mark and Melissa. Typically, these discussions were general starting points, and with appropriate implementation of the CoupleCEO framework in the days and weeks to come, they would see significant improvement in the foundation of their relationship.

Intimacy Is Good for Your Health

"Because we try and tie together the different pieces of the puzzle for you, let's point out some of the health benefits, in addition to everything else we've discussed, that have been clinically proved by having a healthy, intimate relationship:

- **Intimacy helps to relieve stress.** A big health benefit of intimacy is lower blood pressure and overall stress reduction, according to researchers from Scotland who reported their findings in the journal of *Biological Psychology*. They studied twenty-four women and twenty-two men, who kept records of their intimate activities. Researchers found that people who had sex responded better to stress than those who abstained. Being a

CoupleCEO can be very stressful, so let's help relieve some of that stress.

- **Intimacy helps to boost your immunity.** Regular lovemaking increases the level of the immune-boosting antibody immunoglobulin A (IgA), which, in turn, makes your body stronger against such illnesses as the common cold and fever. A Wilkes University study showed that those who had sex once or twice a week had higher levels of IgA than others.

- **Intimacy provides a more sound sleep.** The same endorphins that help you de-stress also can relax your mind and body, priming you for slumber, says Cindy M. Meston, PhD, director of the Sexual Psychophysiology Laboratory at the University of Texas at Austin and coauthor of *Why Women Have Sex*. Getting enough sleep also has been linked to a host of other health benefits, such as a healthy weight and better blood pressure. I have nights that I wake up with my mind reeling about work ideas, but that rarely happens if my sleep was preceded by a nice romantic tryst.

- **Intimacy improves heart health.** A twenty-year-long British study shows that men who had sex two or more times a week were half as likely to have a fatal heart attack as men who had sex less than once a month. And although some older folks may worry that sex could cause a stroke, the study found no link between how often men had sex and how likely they were to have a stroke."

The two CoupleCEOs raised their glasses as Scott and Heidi proposed a toast.

"May you always look at each other and enjoy your togetherness, forever and a day," Scott said.

Mark wrapped his arm around Melissa and squeezed her gently. Scott and Heidi shared a smile as they watched approvingly.

"You know, being intimate is really a crucial part of a happy, satisfied relationship," Scott reminded. "It's the glue that keeps everything together, really. In fact, it's really the glue that holds *all* of the other pieces together. Remember that the magic of being a CoupleCEO is that together, you can accomplish anything you set out to do. And by applying that glue consistently to your relationship, that intimacy that brings it all together, the strength and power of that connection can move the world. And you will discover the beauty that comes with fulfilling your dreams, together."

THE WORDS OF INTIMACY

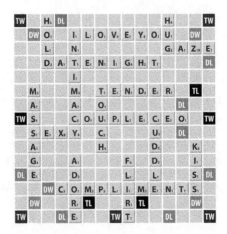

Chapter 9

LIVE THE DREAM

We know what we are, but know not what we may be.

—William Shakespeare

Scott stood at the bow and guided the anchor safely back into the anchor well. As he walked back into the cockpit, Mark had a question waiting.

"So is this your retirement plan, Scott?" asked Mark. "Take the sailboat and go explore the world?"

"Well, I don't really look at it as a retirement plan, more of a life plan," said Scott, grinning. "Heidi and I enjoy incorporating our work into our lifestyle, so I envision we'll keep sailing and providing solutions as we sail the seven seas," Scott laughed, enjoying his alliteration.

Your Business Bull's-Eye "You should ideally create a strategy to do what you're good at, do something that interests you, do something the market wants, and do something that is sustainable. We call it the Business Bull's-Eye." Scott drew a diagram on a piece of paper, with four quadrants—each representing one of the four requirements he spoke about. In the middle, he drew a big bull's-eye, marking the intersection of the four quadrants.

Business Bull's Eye

"That should really be everyone's goal. Figuring out how you can get to that bull's-eye should be a constant navigation tool to make sure you're heading down the right road. For example, Heidi and I enjoy sailing, and we're effective in working with CoupleCEOs to share a framework for their life and help them connect their pieces. So we have chosen to do something that interests us—inspiring entrepreneurial couples. We believe we're pretty good at it. We recognize that the market needs us to take our message and as a business, we will share it with other couple entrepreneurs."

"So you've built a business model that incorporates all of these aspects?" asked Mark.

"Yes, our model, The CoupleCEO™ Framework, was developed to provide couples with the educational experience that will show them how to visualize and realize their full potential in their shared world. By incorporating successful and sustainable strategies, your business and your relationship strengths can be leveraged into a richly fulfilled lifestyle. We bring it all together to help you tailor a complete life where all of the pieces fit. But remember that this framework has grown the business far beyond just Heidi and me working it day to day. Remember that you need to look at your business model as something you can walk away from, and it still produces revenue for you. That's the real bull's-eye, isn't it?"

"Wow!" Mark exclaimed. "That's so true. You know, I've said for years that I'd love for Melissa and me to travel more and see parts of the world that have so many places to explore. I've always been great at uncovering unique items to sell wherever we go. But we have this business, Melissa grew up with it, and it seems to just root us in deeper and deeper. People talk about their spouse as the ball and chain. In my case, Melissa is not the ball and chain; it's our business that makes me feel that way."

"But you've said that the greatest potential in the business is to go online and tap into a world of customers who are looking for the uniqueness that you bring to what you sell in the store, right?" questioned Scott.

"Exactly," replied Mark. "We constantly hear from customers that we have a truly unique offering of items that they haven't found elsewhere in their travels."

"Well, maybe that's your Business Bull's-Eye," Scott said. "Maybe you combine traveling the world in search of unique items to sell with an online store that can attract people from other parts of the world. You can make your travels like Anthony Bourdain does with food, and maybe even create an online video show out of it. Get the Travel Channel to pick it up."

"That's a fantastic idea," Melissa said excitedly. "I've never really made a paradigm shift from my parents' general store to something truly global. But you're right. The technology and our creativity are certainly up to such a task."

"Creating your strategy for your future needs to focus on where your business is heading and making sure it falls in the center of that Business Bull's-Eye," reminded Heidi. "This is going to be the ship you sail as a CoupleCEO to sustain your ambitions and dreams. It has to grow with you both, and remain fun and interesting and, above all, profitable. That's the major key to sustainability."

"That's right," Scott explained. "Sustainable strategies involve managing several objectives:

- Maintaining a pulse on your supply chains so you can continue to produce your inventory.
- Understanding your competitive forces so you can track new entry into your market and potentially create effective barriers to entry.

- Interpreting market demand forces so you can stay abreast of what your market segment wants and needs, as well as discovering new segments to expand into.

- Building business systems and procedures to control the processes behind your business. Remember when we discussed Ray Kroc's approach to building system-wide standards in his business? Give your business the sustainability to run itself without your needing to be at the helm. It's like my autopilot on the boat!"

Succession Planning

"Creating your Business Bull's-Eye definitely puts you on the right path in heading toward your financial future," Heidi said. "But let's not forget about the many other fundamental principles that form the proper foundation. Remember, Scott, it's like our house example. You've got to have the proper foundation, right?"

"Exactly," responded Scott. "One vital component to establishing that proper foundation is succession planning. It could be a family business transitioning from one generation to the next, like your family, Melissa, or identifying the key leadership to 'hand the torch' to for running the business, or maybe just facilitating the appropriate exit strategy in selling the business to the right buyer. All of these scenarios require strategic planning to maximize both your profits as well as your family well-being.

"Understand that there are many acceptable valuation methods in quantifying the true value of a business. The specific industry, the size of the business, and even the circumstances of the sale of a business all play a role. A clear understanding of what the buyer is purchasing is vital to the proper valuation.

For example, is the management/ownership team remaining in place through a transition or earn-out period? Does the business have valuable intangible assets, such as trademarks or patents? Is there a large potential of future prospects in the market segment? Are the key systems and processes documented? Will there be seller financing involved? A couple of business valuation methods are:

- **The asset-based valuation**—This is determined by the total value of the company's tangible and intangible assets. Of course, this method neglects the future earning potential of the company.
- **The earnings multiplier valuation**—Utilizing a specific multiple for an industry, this method would involve valuing a company based on its earning or net income. Basically, the purchaser is buying the earnings of the company for the number of years represented by the multiplier. Another way of expressing this valuation is through a cap rate.
  - o   For example, if a business generates twenty thousand dollars annually, and has an earnings multiplier of five, five times earnings means that it is worth one hundred thousand dollars. Another way to express it is to say that the business has a 20 percent cap rate, meaning that the buyer will receive a 20 percent return on his investment of one hundred thousand dollars.
- **The discounted cash flow valuation**—Depending on the future earnings of the company, perhaps with an

organization poised for growth over the next five years, this method would discount the next five years of *future projected earnings* back to a present-day discounted amount, based on a cost of capital percentage.

"As you can see, uncovering the true value of your business can yield significance to your exit strategies," Scott reminded.

"According to the Family Business Confidence Survey conducted in 2012 by Elizabethtown College, the amount of focus given to strategic planning and succession planning has a direct correlation to the size of the family business. For example, the majority of family businesses without strategic and succession planning are small companies with gross sales of less than one hundred million dollars. As for first-generation businesses, only one-fourth of them had plans in place. But even though only a small percentage had a formal plan in place, 95 percent expressed some degree of confidence that the family will remain in control of the management of the business."

"Interesting, isn't it?" Heidi remarked. "Remember the Pricewaterhouse study that concluded similar findings? In fact, it pointed out that 40 percent of family businesses said they intended to pass ownership and management to the next generation. But more than half of them were unsure whether the next generation could do it successfully."

"The reality is that succession planning is not typically on the entrepreneur's radar screen, but it is important and needs to be addressed so as not to cause a bump in the road someday," Scott insisted. "Think of some of the issues that can arise, and they do:

- **Entitlement**—Family business members believe that no matter how they act, the business is there to serve them.
- **Nepotism**—This is the hiring or advancing of personnel based solely on family relationships.
- **Founderitis**—This is when a founder believes that he or she is the business's only capable manager, leading to a lack of appreciation for anyone else in the organization being capable of succeeding him or her. This is indicative of a company that lacks the proper systems and processes.

"It's important for the business to answer the question of whether it is going to be a family business or a business family. Will they run the business like a family, or like a business that is owned by a family? As a CoupleCEO, the answer to this question most certainly will predict the future success of the business as well as the foundation of your financial future," Scott concluded.

"Another fundamental principal that forms the proper foundation is your focus on liquidity," Heidi began. "One of our business partners, a wealth management expert, asks an important question to all of his entrepreneurial clients. He asks, 'How big a check can they write tomorrow?' It allows the message of liquidity to be drilled down to its lowest level. Someone can look very wealthy on paper but face bankruptcy immediately. Just remember, cash is always your best friend!

"Remember that cash provides opportunity. And if you have cash, people will find you. Jack Welch, the legendary CEO of General Electric, prayed for a good recession because he had cash. Warren Buffett is always looking for opportunities with his cash. According to *The Wall Street Journal*, Berkshire Hathaway had about forty billion dollars by the third quarter of 2013. Apple had about $147 billion in the same year. You can bet they are always looking for opportunities with that cash. Now, we don't expect you to have the cash reserves of a Berkshire Hathaway or an Apple, but you must understand the importance of it."

"Remember that true wealth isn't about large homes, fancy yachts, or expensive jewelry," Scott reminded. "It's really about discretionary time. It's about having the time to follow your dreams. It's about taking care of those around you. By following a strategy of proper financial planning, you can continue to invest in yourselves to create a financial freedom that defines your idea of wealth. And what is that amount?

"Let me give you an example of how this works. First, create a budget for your lifestyle; we'll call it 'your number'—the amount of after-tax annual cash flow each year your family needs to enjoy its lifestyle. You can even do it by the month if it's easier to calculate, but don't forget those annual expenses, such as insurance and taxes. There are the fixed expenses, of course—the utilities, mortgage, and so on, and there are the other expenses, the variable ones, the dinners out, the kids' soccer, music lessons, the vacations, and the unexpected ones, such as home repairs. The goal is to focus on your cash flow and eliminate any fixed obligations that you can."

"You mean like paying off your mortgage?" Mark asked.

"Exactly. Do you have enough cash liquidity to pay off your mortgage? Then, take your annual earnings, any investments, and so on, and figure out the net figure after all expenses in the budget, and see what the amount is. That's the amount that you should be investing in yourself to eventually fund your lifestyle.

In other words, this fixed inflow of income should be gradually replaced over time with enough accumulated capital invested at a low return to fund your lifestyle."

Mark chimed in, "So let's say we have $120,000 left over annually after covering our lifestyle overhead. You're saying that the $120,000 accumulates over time to eventually fund our lives when we're not working anymore? And we don't count on an eventual windfall gain from selling our business some day?"

"Exactly," Heidi answered. "Because that profit in yourselves of $120,000 annually can go a long way toward your financial freedom. You are investing in yourself. This is your annual personal profit, accumulating to arrive at a place of independence. What everyone really needs to figure out for himself or herself is what does that independence mean to you? What does your life look like when you have the money to do whatever you want to in life, and the money is not funded by your labor? If you could do anything you wanted to do, what would it be? And, as a couple, is it something that you both agree on? Our children will tell you that we will be sailing parts of the world later in life, and most of our friends would probably tell you the same thing.

"You know, money isn't really anything without knowing your destination, your goal, or your dream. Money is only a tool for bringing things of real value into existence. This is why we find it so important to know what you are searching for in life, what both of you are searching for, and to find the commonality. By focusing on your Business Bull's-Eye, you are creating that perfect engine to get you down the road to where you ultimately want to be. You are creating your required cash flows, but more importantly, you're living a satisfying life that places you both in balance."

"The thing we hate to hear about most of all is the couple who work for years in something they don't enjoy, something they're not really good at, or something the market doesn't accept very well—the couple who haven't found their Bull's-Eye," Scott lamented.

"Many families go into a business without even considering how this business will fit into their lifestyle," Heidi said. "Before starting a business, people should ask themselves if they want a lifestyle business or a performance business. A lifestyle business has three to twelve employees and typically grosses between one million and two million dollars. A performance business begins as a small to medium business, has fewer than fifty employees, and grosses closer to six million dollars. Part of the reason to ask yourself this question prior to starting your business is because the lifestyle attitude is to earn enough money to live a comfortable life and to have time to enjoy the lifestyle you have created. A performance business requires more energy to run the business and is usually being positioned to sell off. These business owners tend to enjoy doing this a few times over their working years. Although it is best to determine this in advance, sometimes halfway through is also a good time to make this determination. And in the case of the CoupleCEO, to make sure the expectation is the same for both of you.

"Life's too short to not realize this much earlier. There are definitely strategies in moving toward financial independence, as I've mentioned, from liquidity strategies to *knowing your number* strategies and then to understanding your personal profit. But the one thing to remember is that someday you'll be rocking on your front porch in your favorite rocking chair, maybe ninety-seven years old, looking back on your life. You don't want to be rocking and regretting things you didn't do with your life, do you? There's a famous quote by Mark Twain that we have in our master bath. It goes like this: 'Twenty years from now you will be more disappointed by the things that you didn't do than by the ones you did do. So throw off the bowlines. Sail away from the safe harbor. Catch the trade winds in your sails. Explore. Dream. Discover.'"

The *Grand Cru* sailed on as the afternoon sky reflected on the rippling waves of the waters beneath. Its crew pondered on the words and the thoughts that contributed to this day. Frameworks and strategies were beginning to be formed. The excitement of these new concepts and fresh ideas left both Mark and Melissa tingling with hope and anticipation. There was a lot to do, but with Scott and Heidi and all that CoupleCEO would help to facilitate, they felt that a new life would be beginning for them when they reached the dry land and stepped onto the docks of the marina. The beauty of a day at sail is that it frees the soul to create, solve, and thrive. The liberating effect of the water produces something magical, giving life to perfect solutions.

Chapter 10

THE ROAD TRAVELED

We're here to put a dent in the universe. Otherwise why else even be here?

—Steve Jobs

The quiet in the sailboat cockpit wasn't revealing everything that was racing through Mark's and Melissa's thoughts. So much to think about, and so much to do . . . . It was exciting and daunting all at once.

Sensing their feelings, Heidi began to summarize. "Well, we've certainly covered a lot today, haven't we?"

Melissa turned to Mark and laughed. "We definitely have, but it's so exciting to just think through all of the possibilities that are at our doorstep. I feel we are stepping into a whole new chapter of our lives. That was not what I expected today. I thought we would get a few tips on a few things in our lives and business. But exploring this framework has actually done everything from getting us to consider taking our business in a whole new direction to making us ask ourselves what our future should look like and how to prepare for it. It is wonderful to see what's possible, but also, it feels a little scary."

Heidi smiled, "Don't worry, what you're feeling is normal. You've both just opened up to seeing things in a whole new light."

"Think of it this way," Scott said. "You've just cleared off your new lot, and now you're getting ready to start building your house. You know what the foundation will look like, and the construction process has started. Just be sure to invite us to the open house when it's completed!"

"Oh, I think we are both looking forward to CoupleCEO helping us build it!" Mark exclaimed.

"Absolutely," Heidi answered. "You know we are there with you every step of the way. In the days and months ahead, our CoupleCEO Acceleration Program will explore all of these concepts in much richer detail. So let's see if we can recap the highlights from today's journey. We explored what makes up a CoupleCEO—the strength of your relationship can bring a unique and powerful force into running your business and your life. And it's that uniqueness that is every CoupleCEO's ultimate strength."

"It's our superhero power," Mark blurted out excitedly.

"That's a good way to look at it," Heidi remarked. "It can be the greatest asset you have, your connection with each other.

Understanding the genetic makeup allows you to accomplish great things in your businesses, your personal lives, your communities, and indeed your legacies. Appreciating the core foundation that is your relationship truly allows you to build great things in your life."

"We definitely see that now, Heidi," Melissa remarked as she took Mark's hand onto her lap.

"One of the many pieces of the puzzle is, of course, time management," Heidi continued. "Managing the balance in your lives among family time, work time, couple time, and definitely alone time—it all takes a lot of discipline and planning, but there are definitely solutions to having the time to get things done in life. But just as you wouldn't start sailing to the Bahamas without a chart onboard, you need to have a map to plan the best out of each twenty-four-hour day. That's why we believe the solution is Priority Planning and Personal Productivity, as we discussed this morning. This good time management planning ultimately will lead to more free time and more creative thinking time to plan for your future."

"That's right, Heidi," Scott continued. "Identifying and charting your priorities are like waypoints on your route. You have to sequentially plot your course and include what is meaningful and important in addressing the needs of each of your obligations—to yourself, your partner, your business, your children, your parents, your community, and your friends. Rather than getting overwhelmed with all of it, simply use the Priority Planning and Personal Productivity as your solution to chart your course. You'll find much smoother sailing as you balance your way through life."

"And that leads us to the second component we talked about today: business strategies," Heidi began. "Remember that understanding your business is the key pillar in building a long-term strategy of success. Understanding who your customers are and why they are attracted to your product or service is vital. Learn how they find you and what they are looking for when they search for you. Do you know what they really want? And do you know what messaging you want to create to have them find you?

"As we identify our personality types and the roles we play in both our business and personal life, we are allowed to excel as a CoupleCEO because we bring together an understanding of our true preferences. It allows us to develop a successful strategy to grow and prosper. We can build our business organizations virtually as we continue to replace ourselves along the way with talented human resources, while never relying on any one single person too much. Remember, your systems and processes should be your major company asset. With these systems in place, your company will always represent what is most important to you, be a reflection of your legacy."

"And as you said, Scott, the technology that exists today to harness your business is amazing," reminded Mark. "I'm glad to know that our technology tool belt is so vast. I'm looking forward to synchronizing our lives a little better so we can focus on the productive things more and let the apps work in the background. I'm also looking forward to receiving your updates on a regular basis because I know these things change constantly."

"Exactly!" Scott exclaimed. "Just keep everything in the cloud, and you'll have it when you need it. Evernote, Skype, Siri, Dropbox—they will all be your new best friends. And don't worry about new solutions that come up over time; we'll make sure you stay abreast of the latest so you can keep your tool belt well-stocked.

"Remember what I said about a business being like a person," reminded Scott. "We need to remember to keep our passion for what we do in the business that we develop, because ultimately, we are a reflection of what we build, what we create, and what legacy we leave behind. You must nurture your business, feeding it with a strategy and intuition that will allow it to prosper. It will take time, sure, but it should be a labor of love because you are building it to take care of you, like building a house to provide you with shelter. The entrepreneur wears his business on his sleeve. He bleeds for it. He feeds it, and he cares for it because he expects great things from it someday."

"I think both of us see great things in store for our business, don't we, Mark?" questioned Melissa.

"Great things to come for our store," agreed Mark. "We're looking forward to working with your team going forward to really make an impact with solutions for our business."

"I really found our discussions on health and fitness very insightful," Melissa added. "Your energy and enthusiasm are contagious!"

"Thanks. We're glad to share it," Heidi said. "You could say that sharing about health and nutrition just makes sense because it allows us to fuel all of the other creativity and energy that go into everything we do. By demonstrating solutions for eating right and staying fit, every CoupleCEO can do amazing things with their lives. To ignore or not stay focused on it would mean to ignore a fundamental pillar of connecting all the pieces, right?"

"Exactly," replied Melissa energetically.

"Understanding what various foods do for us is like knowing what gas goes into your car," Heidi continued. "As we understand these dynamics, we're just following what nature always intended. Do we think that processed foods and refined sugars do anyone any good, other than the companies that make them? The more we try to eliminate them from our diet, the better off we are in the long run."

"Just remember the simple concept of the plate having one-third protein and two-thirds colorful carbohydrates, such as vegetables and fruits," Scott reminded. "A little bit of fat, like nuts or olive oil, and you are good to go. Just watch out for the starchy carbs, such as breads, pastas, potatoes, or rice. Keep the balance of proteins, carbohydrates, and fats at every meal, and don't stress it. If you sometimes screw up, don't worry; the next meal is around the corner, and you can get back to correcting it."

"Try not to think of this as dieting; just think of it as eating right," Heidi added. "That's a solution you can live by. And we'll keep you posted on new recipes we find along the way."

"Don't forget to add our standby favorites too," reminded Scott. "We have a lot of time in the kitchen, Heidi and I, including our weekly Sunday night dinner with an extended family of usually twenty or so."

Heidi chimed in, "And we enjoy it too. Oh, and don't forget about the water. Keep drinking plenty of it, always."

"Well, I'm looking forward to getting on a regular exercise routine," Mark announced. "And I plan on Melissa and I being the motivators for each other, not the nags."

"We're going to direct you to some exercise routines that can be as little as ten minutes a day," Heidi said. "You can view it from your smartphone, smart TV, or tablet device. It's like having a fitness instructor in your own home, on the road in a hotel, or anywhere you want. Following along with these workouts is definitely a healthy solution anyone can pick up and take with him or her. I suggest doing them together, like Scott and I do."

"Sounds like the perfect segue into reviewing our intimacy discussion, Heidi," laughed Scott. "What do you both remember the most from our talk?"

"No business talk," Mark blurted out.

"Have intimate moments daily," Melissa added.

"Well, some excellent takeaways," laughed Heidi. "Additionally, let's remember that moments of intimacy can continue the sparkle throughout the many moments of your day.

"Remember the touches, the looks, the shared experiences that only mean something to each other, but make the most out of each of you together as a couple. Remember that each of you and both of you must search out the opportunities to share those moments of intimacy. Make them random, make them unique, make them special, and share them often."

"Sometimes everything around you can fade away when the two of you have a certain moment," Scott explained. "The world can be spinning a million miles a minute, but if both of you just stop and share something together, it's as if everything else just fades away and ceases to matter. Remember that the 'superhero strength' comes from your unique relationship. We must continue to find ways to nurture that relationship. The solution is to make those intimate moments you both create be the glue that keeps that uniqueness strong and powerful."

Melissa smiled as she looked at Mark. "This is what we are looking forward to the most, seeing that the small things we do together really are a lot larger than we ever realized before. Like those day hikes that we used to take every Saturday. And going to those farmers markets afterward and getting those vegetables for the night's stir-fry. We just stopped doing that. . . . I'm not sure why."

"I guess we just get into a pattern, and we didn't even realize we had stopped doing it," Mark concluded.

"Think of these moments like when you're exercising," Heidi reminded. "You have to work new muscle groups and not get into the same pattern of exercise all the time. Shake it up, and try new things, have new experiences, go new ways. Remember Robert Frost's poem:

> Two roads diverged in a yellow wood, and I—
> I took the one less traveled by,
> And that has made all the difference.

"When we don't work different muscle groups, we don't obtain the proper effects of exercise. It's the same for our relationship— try new things together on the menu of life, and you'll be amazed with the outcomes."

Relax and Enjoy It

The western horizon glowed with the setting sun spreading her colors across the open sky. The *Grand Cru* rounded the breakwater of the marina as Scott slowed the engine to an idle. He expertly eased *Grand Cru* and her passengers back into the slip. The seagulls were making their late sunset rounds on the calm waters. The passengers just sat quietly, taking it all in.

"Taking the road less traveled has made all the difference for us," Scott remarked. "I couldn't think of anything else I would rather be doing right now than exactly this," he added as he propped up his feet onto the bulkhead and enjoyed a deep breath of sea air.

"Like I said before, you've got to find your Bull's-Eye. Life's just too short to ignore the quest. I wish sometimes we could share this message with more people. I mean, as a couple, the world has so much to offer and so much to explore, together. So it's really about getting all of the pieces in place to make it happen, to make them happen, or, I guess, to just make life happen.

"When I look back on when Heidi and I came together as a couple, back on that Haleakalā Crater at sunrise, when I proposed to her, and luckily she accepted . . . that was the beginning of our road traveled. We have gone down that road, we have journeyed some paths that were bumpy and some paths that were scenic, and we've learned along the way.

"A favorite expression of ours is that it's not the destination, but the journey that's most important. Our journey as a couple has always been about what makes our life so rich with memories, experiences, and life lessons. What we are building together is documentation of our journey, our 'ship's log,' and our passion is to share our lessons with others, to share solutions and explore strategies in an effort to promote that superhero strength called Couple Power."

"Scott and I have always shared this passion, and that's why I said yes to him that morning in Hawaii," Heidi said, smiling. "You know, it's the unique creative energy of entrepreneurship and the powerful force of a relationship that is a formative combination. By harnessing all of that together, the world can see a lot of benefit. That positive change is a solution that we feel everyone can embrace."

"That's why we were initially drawn to both of you and the concept of the CoupleCEO," Melissa admitted. "Mark and I have always known that our relationship could build great things in our life. But sometimes the destination just needs to be in clearer focus. We just needed some solutions in putting the pieces together to get to where we wanted to be, as a couple, as a business, and really where we want to eventually be."

"See, that's the journey you're talking about," Scott answered with a smile. "If you get too caught up with where you need to be, you lose sight of the fact that getting there, your shared journey, is really what it's all about. Just focus on your relationship, and you will continually be amazed with the positive energy that will permeate into the rest of your life.

"One of the best things my parents ever taught me was to just *relax and enjoy it.* At the time, I didn't really understand what they were trying to teach me. However, in my youth, I seemed to always look ahead more and worry about what was to come, rather than simply enjoying the *now.* Enjoying the now is enjoying your relationship, your family, and together, you have a lot of great things to accomplish.

"Melissa, I think you and Mark will begin to enjoy your journey more, as together you continue to strengthen your relationship as a CoupleCEO and find the paths that will build those satisfactions in your life. As you continue to implement your solutions to improve your business, your health, your intimacy, and your management of time, that journey will build momentum and purpose. As you know where you want to be heading, the ride to get there is a blast. We recommend that you both hop onboard and enjoy the ride!"

"And don't worry," Heidi assured them. "We'll be with you every step of the way to make it the ride of your life, literally!" They all laughed as they started to collect their belongings. Mark and Melissa slowly walked to the bow of the sailboat, holding hands as they looked out onto the water.

"Turn around for your portrait," Scott insisted. He framed the couple as they leaned back into the bowsprit and gave a relaxed smile back to the camera. "This is to remember this moment for the rest of your lives, okay?" He smiled and gave Melissa a warm hug, and firmly shook Mark's hand with both of his.

"Well, I think this is the beginning of a beautiful friendship," Scott said with his best Humphrey Bogart accent.

Mark and Melissa laughed as they stepped onto the dock, taking their bags from Scott as he handed them over the lifelines.

"Hope you enjoyed today's journey," Heidi said.

"The journey has just begun," Melissa said, smiling. "And we're looking forward to it tremendously."

With that, the couple kissed, held hands, and walked away, past the other moored boats in the marina. With the sunset in front of them, they were in fact walking into the sunset. But Scott and Heidi knew that with the journey Mark and Melissa were embarking upon, they were now enjoying their new sunrise.

ABOUT THE AUTHORS

 Scott and Heidi Shimberg began their story on the top of a mountain in Hawaii at sunrise. With the morning dawn, and a proposal for marriage, Scott and Heidi have been looking upwards ever since. Over the past 20 years as a CoupleCEO, they have built, developed, and sold over a quarter of a billion dollars of real estate through their entrepreneurial efforts. While doing this they have enjoyed giving back through community non-profit projects and living a lifestyle complete with family, fun, and passion.

Their journey is similar to that of many entrepreneurs, from experiencing the highs of real-estate successes to the lows of housing crashes, the fears of financial failure, and the daily worries of every business owner. Through the wealth of their experiences, and by utilizing the foundational strength of their relationship, they have been able to create a profound impact on their entrepreneurial pursuits, on their community, and in the lives of their family and friends.

They are passionate about sharing with others their strategies of balancing business profitability with a fulfilled relationship. They know that with the right framework, a business and relationship can coexist and thrive. Scott and Heidi enjoy being a CoupleCEO. Their desire is to bring to life what every CoupleCEO deserves—a profitable business and a passionate relationship.

Scott and Heidi live in Tampa, Florida, where Scott was born and raised. They stay busy raising their three sons, Joshua, Seth, and Adam. You can spot them on the weekends at soccer games or sailing the local waters. On Sundays they are gathered around the dining room table with their extended family, a tradition they are proud to have instilled in their family.

CONTINUE
THE JOURNEY
WITH US

Join our CoupleCEO Community!
Go to

Coupleceo.com/bookoffer

to receive a free introductory membership
into the CoupleCEO Community.

Appendix

PERSONALITY TYPE
WHEEL SUMMARY

Inspirer

ENFPs believe anything is possible. They thrive in a world of brainstorming possibilities. They are curious about everything. New things fascinate them, yet they don't like to focus on details. The fun is in the idea, rather than the implementation. They thrive on being around people. They work best in groups, can have a tendency towards procrastination, and can be easily distracted. They dislike routines and schedules but love involvement. Their distractions by new opportunities or social interaction may interfere with productivity. They are committed and care about their long-lasting circle of friendship, yet others may sometimes feel overwhelmed by their enthusiasm. They crave harmony in their interactions, seek participation, and excel as inspirational consensus builders.

Executive

ENTJs are natural leaders who proactively organize their lives and their work based on their clear, efficient standards and logical beliefs. They cannot *not* lead. They love a persuasive argument and value others who are knowledgeable and speak their mind. Their love of learning provides curious motivation to pursue a better way. They have a high need for achievement based on their standards, not others'. Often they do not realize the need for giving praise or feedback to others. They will become impatient with inefficiency and errors. Hardworking themselves, they will expect the same from others. Their "workaholic" tendencies may require more efforts to balance work with family.

Visionary

ENTPs see the big picture and want to jump right into it. They enjoy inventing, creating, and envisioning the plans more than seeing to the detailed implementation. Very flexible and adaptable, they will be bored without the challenge of multiple projects. They tend to have a high need for autonomy and lack of structure. They are students of life, learning new concepts and insights to create and promote their inspirations. They want to see their visions materialize but may lack the ability to follow through. Always the optimist, if something should make sense, then eventually it will. They enjoy a playful debate, a creative spark, seeing possible futures, picturing potentials, and delegating to others.

Mechanic

ISTPs are action oriented and thrive on being able to troubleshoot an issue by gathering their tools and fixing it. They have an intrinsic ability to understand how things work. Their pragmatic approach focuses them on getting the task done without worrying about theoretical possibilities. They have no fear of the impossible and want to figure it out now. They are cool and unemotional and communicate with the least amount of words needed. They admire and relate well to people who are skilled and respond quickly to problems in a logical manner.

Caregiver

ESFJs give of themselves to others and are very easy to get to know. They provide an immediate connection with others. They share a lot about themselves, feeling deeply emotional, friendly, and outgoing to those around them, enjoying a sense of belonging. They make sure the needs of others are met, putting others' interests before their own with a conscientious sense of duty and responsibility. It is important to them that they are well liked by others, and seen as reliable and dependable. Stability and a familiar routine are important. Embracing change is difficult. They are detail minded with great memory recall, actively organizing and helping people, events, and things. Keepers of preserving traditions, customs, and celebrations, they maintain the practical stability and harmony of both home and work.

Protector

INFJs are protectors of the cause, the vision, or the ideal that is their driving force. In the service to others, with their dreams and plans, they will inspire, listen, and create. They need their work to help others and to advance their vision. They are most comfortable in the creative idea stage, but are ultimately driven by the vision. They are content to work behind the scenes. They attract those around them through their inspiration and their keen sense to provide praise to others. It is important that the people they surround themselves with are harmonious.

Entertainer

ESFPs are natural performers, loyal friends, eager to help others, and great companions. They tend to see the "best" in everyone, seeking new immediate experiences and learning by doing. They live for the moment, enjoy having fun, and are enjoyable to be around. They have a good sense of people and their physical surroundings, and can gather a group together to create excitement and energy. They thrive on active social interaction, opportunities, choices, and flexibility. They have a strong sensory awareness. They enjoy living in the moment and in the middle of things. Highly averse to conflict, they go out of their way to avoid it. Occasionally they say what others want to hear to avoid conflict.

Thinker

INTPs are lifelong learners and strategists with a logical, analytical approach to their personal and professional lives. They are infinitely curious about new ideas and approaches to solving problems. They seek knowledge for the sake of knowledge; they love to theorize and abhor redundancy. They can get so caught up "in "their head" that they ignore things around them and time can pass them by. They are quite skeptical, as it is natural for them to question everything. They trust logical reasoning and do not understand emotional responses.

Guardian

ESTJs take their responsibilities seriously, efficiently organizing and analyzing their present world and getting the jobs at hand done quickly and done right. Productivity is their goal, with a strong understanding of the facts. They are the ideal project manager, complete with agendas and schedules. They have a responsible and decisive take-charge attitude, are highly competitive, and have a strong need to be in control. They perform best in highly structured environments. Tried and true traditional methods are more agreeable than experimental methods with change. Maintaining order and loyalty is paramount to their organizations, groups, family, and culture.

Doer

ESTPs are active participants in all aspects of their lives, full of energy and ready to go. With a friendly, casual, spontaneous, and easygoing manner, their focus is on the experiences of life, not the organizing or judging of it. As astute observers, when they are paying attention, they notice everything around them, while not relying much on the theoretical or abstract. They need their freedom and are uncomfortable with excessive structure. They learn by doing and live for the moment. They want to get things done; they are bored by analysis and talking about it. They attract others around them by their activity and enjoyment of the present.

Scientist

INTJs possess valuable insights through tenacious attention into their inner world and ideas. Logical analysis dominates their life. Their focus is on long-term, big-picture, strategic concepts and plans, and they are likely to work alone or in small, trusted groups. They are extremely confident with their ideas and trust their insight and their ideal solution, while constantly exploring scenarios to find the right answer. They are constantly seeking improvement, both from themselves and from the concept or system they are focusing on. They will become bored without challenge; however, they have a desire for independence and autonomy to discover, innovate, and achieve.

Idealist

INFPs seek harmony in everything they do in their personal and professional lives. It is important to them that their actions are congruent with their beliefs. They are very aware of the feelings and concerns of those around them and seem to know exactly what to say at the right time to express empathy and concern. They are curious about the world around them and tend to be avid readers who communicate best in the written word. Also, they are often lovers of the arts. They are best working for a bigger cause: "bigger than life" is perfect for them. They get frustrated with mundane, routine work. Due to their quest for harmony, they will avoid conflict as long as possible.

Nurturer

ISFJs are dependable and focused on doing what needs to be done. They are pragmatic with a tremendous amount of common sense. They base their decisions on previous history and have excellent memories. They have an innate ability to remember dates and events, especially as it pertains to their family. They are very good listeners, eager to help people, and have a natural kinship with children. They seek stability and certainty in their lives, and are most comfortable in familiar situations. In an adverse situation, they will find it difficult to communicate.

Artist

ISFPs live in the present and are spontaneous with their actions; they epitomize the term "living in the moment." They communicate with others through expression and artistry rather than words. They perform best in crisis mode and are energized by action not theory. Routine and rigidity bore them; they do not appreciate structure and can find themselves overwhelmed by complex, long-range projects. They need harmony in their environment and will expend energy to avoid confrontation.

Giver

ENFJs are satisfied when they can bring out the positive potential in other people. They are inspiring, caring, empathetic, compassionate, and friendly to large social networks that seek them out. Their intuition allows them to understand people's feelings, and their motivation is to make them happy, to make them feel good, and to inspire them to reach their goals. They are excellent communicators, both one-on-one and in front of audiences. They can also be very loyal followers. Their energy comes from their interaction with people, and they will put others' needs before their own. They plan, organize, and create networks, connecting others with similar interests together. They tend to "wear their hearts on their sleeves."

Duty Fulfiller

ISTJs feel a strong sense of duty and are intensely committed to their organizations, families, and relationships. They are responsible. Facts and details are central in their lives. They focus on getting the job done and working methodically by using proven ways. They do not want to try untested ways of doing things. "If it works, why change it?" Not easily distracted, they will make the tough calls, not concerned about how it will look to others. They say what they mean and mean what they say, doing what needs to be done. They love to use a planner or calendar as a tool to plan what needs to be done and track what has been accomplished, working efficiently. Disorganization as well as interruptions will distract them. They enjoy their routines, are straightforward in their communications, and controlled in the display of their emotions.

Printed in the USA
CPSIA information can be obtained
at www.ICGtesting.com
JSHW082345140824
68134JS00020B/1886

9 781630 472887